A CONCISE GUIDE TO THE LEARNING ORGANIZATION

The Mike Pedler Library

Developing people and organizations

General Editor: Dr Mike Pedler

Books published simultaneously in this series:

Reg Revans
ABC of Action Learning

Nancy M. Dixon
Dialogue at Work

Mike Pedler and Kath Aspinwall
A Concise Guide to the Learning Organization

Rennie Fritchie and Malcolm Leary
Resolving Conflicts in Organizations

*Would you like to receive regular information about forthcoming
new books in the Mike Pedler Library? Would you like to
send us your comments about the book you have read? If so, we would
be very pleased to hear from you.*

Lemos & Crane
20 Pond Square
Highgate Village
London N6 6BA
England
Tel   +44(0)181 348 8263
Fax   +44(0)181 347 5740
Email admin@lemos.demon.co.uk

A Concise Guide to the Learning Organization

MIKE PEDLER AND KATH ASPINWALL

Lemos&Crane

This edition first published in Great Britain 1998
Lemos&Crane
20 Pond Square
Highgate
London N6 6BA

ISBN 1-898001-43-X

A CIP catalogue record for this book is available from the British Library.

Designed and typeset by DAP Ltd, London.
Printed and Bound by Redwood Books, Trowbridge.

Contents

INTRODUCTION TO THE LIBRARY

"All learning is for the sake of action, and all action for the sake of friendship." John Macmurray

At the end of centuries and especially millennia, all manner of prophecies break out and gain hold in the public imagination. The world of business and management is no exception to this law as it entertains a great variety of excited ideas for dealing with the better ordering of business and corporate affairs in the face of the supposed end of certainty and, with this, the arts of prediction and strategic planning. In their place we are offered notions of paradox, of chaos and boundlessness, of multiple dilemmas and complexity theory. And these are merely at the "softer" end; at the other there is much old wine in new bottles as the nostrums of Taylorism and Fordism suffuse the apparently novel re-engineering and quality movements.

The value of learning

To be responsive to change, a child, adult, organization, even a society, must be adept at learning. Learning is the means not only of acquiring new knowledge and skill but also of making sense of our lives - individually and collectively - in increasingly fragmented times. We may not know "the how" of this or that, but we can go on hopefully in pursuit of learning a way through. In the absence of a plan, a blueprint for success, we can learn our way forward, growing in confidence as to what we can do and in who we are, making our own path.

For organizations, with an average lifespan of 40 years and declining, learning has become essential for survival (De Geus). Organizational learning has also been suggested as the only sustainable source of competitive advantage (Senge) and the single most important quality which can be developed and traded (Garratt).

At community or society level new efforts at collaborative action and learning in public forums to tackle the "wicked" problems of poverty, inequality, pollution, crime and public safety look so much more relevant than the old questions of left or right, public or private, electoral democracy or entrepreneurial leadership.

For societies, communities, organizations and individuals the questions are similar: how can we develop those things which we do best so as to be able to trade, exchange, learn, whilst not shutting our eyes to the downsides, shadows, problems and consequences? How can we release energy, potential, self-reliability and active citizenship and build wealth, well-being, collective security, welfare, public services and generally improve the quality of our lives?

A Learning Society?

In an era characterised by large organizations and complexity, it has become plain that individual learning, however impressive, cannot alone resolve problems in relationships - be they at personal, team or organizational level. Equally, it is becoming clear that even the very best of our organizations, private or public, cannot alone resolve the intractable issues of communities and societies. The idea of the "learning organization" is a recognition of, and one response to, the limits of individual learning. But more is needed; there are urgent tasks to hand which go beyond the scope and remit of any single organization or coalition of agencies. As touched on above, these issues demand the organization of action and learning in a different context, and one which is scarcely yet glimpsed, yet alone grasped. In such an ideal collaboration as a Learning Society, there is:

- The freedom to learn - or not to learn - for individuals.

- An organizational aim to support the learning of all members and stakeholders and a desire to transform the organization, as a whole and when appropriate, in creating new products, services and relationships.

- A social drive to provide equality of opportunity for learning to all citizens, at least partly in order that they might contribute to that society being a good place to live in.

The links in this collaborative ideal can be represented diagramatically as follows:

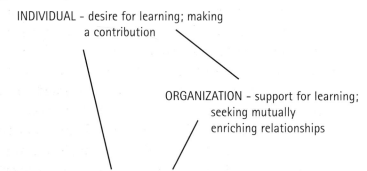

INDIVIDUAL - desire for learning; making a contribution

ORGANIZATION - support for learning; seeking mutually enriching relationships

COMMUNITY/SOCIETY - equal opportunities for learning; providing a good place to live

This manifesto is of course a re-interpretation of old revolutionary aspirations - Liberty (for individuals), the ruling value of Fraternity for organizations, and a duty of Equality of treatment and opportunity in the social sphere.

To each of these we hope to make a contribution, without being confined or encompassed by ideas of personal self-development, or of organizational change, learning, and transformation, nor yet by those of community development or social policy. If a book focuses on, say, organizational processes, then it also keeps an eye on the personal and social development aspects; if it is primarily aimed at the self-development of individuals, then this is in the context of working in organizations and living in society.

The books in the Library are concerned with learning and action on such pressing issues facing us as people working in organizations, living in communities, cities and societies. And whilst there is no single philosophy here, there is an implied criticism of the economic and cultural consensus which underlies much business and management literature in particular. There are challenges here for those who tend to assume that our future rests on the "roll out" of global, information-based capitalism supported by the spread of liberalism and democracy. There is support here for those who question whether individual or organizational development aimed at "high performance" or "excellence" inevitably leads only to desirable outcomes. Here, the irony of the self-proclaimed "learning organization" that is still not a healthy place for people to work in or to live next to, is noted. Here is an aspiration to engage our "best and brightest" and our talent for organizing with some of the really difficult and intractable issues facing us. Above all, we seek to be inclusive and to sustain and support all those trying to learn new things in order to act differently in pursuit of friendship.

Beyond ideas to useful action

Because action and learning require more than just good ideas, the Library is characterised by two more "laws of three". In terms of content, each book contains:

- *educational input* - ideas of substance that you need to know about.

- *invitations to action* - at various points it is suggested that you need to stop and to actually do something with the ideas in order to learn.

- *ethical or political elements* - being an honest colleague, doing the "right thing", seeking good purposes or responding to difficult tasks and circumstances usually imply ethical dilemmas or struggle and perhaps the need for moral support in action and learning.

In terms of pitch or level, though they aim to be attractive and accessible, these books are not "easy reads". Not content with theories and suspicious of easy answers, tools and techniques, these books offer a middle ground of active methods and approaches to the problems and questions posed. Here is an invitation to self-confrontation for the reader. Aware of the complexity and of the questions to which there are no answers, nevertheless there are ways forward, structures to use, directions to follow in order to engage your own energies, the ingenuity of colleagues and the aspirations of customers or those you serve in order to learn your way through. You can't put such a book down without at least thinking of doing something differently.

Mike Pedler

1 Introduction

"If we are to survive – individually or as companies, or as a country – we must create a tradition of 'learning companies'. Every company must be a 'learning company'."[1]

For leaders and managers facing unprecedented and unpredictable change, the learning organization has become an urgent quest. It offers a vision of an organization that is able to flex, adapt and be responsive to change. Learning is vital for today's organizations as their trading conditions become ever more volatile and bewildering. Learning, in individuals, teams and the organization as a whole, offers a way forward – if it can be understood, embraced and harnessed towards strategic purpose. A definition of the learning organization is that it is:

> "an organization that facilitates the learning of all its members and consciously transforms itself and its context."[2]

It is not enough for a company to do lots of training – a training company is not the same thing as a learning company. Learning organizations are very concerned about the learning of all their people but all this can be wasted unless it is harnessed in learning at the whole organization level.

This book is for those who feel that their people and their organizations contain a great deal of unrealised potential – and who also want to set about releasing it. It is for those who want to create organizations that are capable of transforming themselves in response to the needs and aspirations of people inside and outside to enrich and sustain the wider world of which they are a part.

Although this is a new field it is one that is developing rapidly. There is no blueprint for the learning organization because all companies have unique histories and collective visions of the future. There are, however, principles, models and approaches that can be adapted and used to enhance your own organization's capacity to learn.

This *Concise Guide to the Learning Organization* offers practical ideas, tools and encouragement to help with the development of your learning organization. It contains:

- Ideas, models and information.

- Case examples and 'snapshots' of organizations working towards becoming learning organizations.

- Applications or practical activities, which you can use to apply the ideas in your own organization.

Chapter 2 explores the idea of the learning organization and explains why it has become part of the vision for so many ambitious enterprises. It argues that the capacity to learn is one of the best guarantors of survival and success in unpredictable times and considers the benefits of thinking of organizations as living organisms. Finally it offers several definitions of the learning organization and an opportunity to generate one to suit your own particular organization.

It is possible to get a sense of what the learning organization might look like. Chapter 3 includes the Eleven Characteristics of the Learning Company (Pedler, Burgoyne and Boydell's model or framework for the learning organization) and contains four case examples of organizations seeking to attain this vision. A questionnaire based on the Eleven Characteristics provides a template to see how your organization matches up and what you could do to improve it.

In answering the question, "How can an organization learn?" it is helpful to start at the level of the individual and Chapter 4 opens with consideration of the nature of learning before moving on to organizational learning. A description of four different kinds or types of learning including organizational learning leads to a discussion of what we mean by organizational learning, including Peter Senge's *Five Disciplines of the Learning Organization*.

The learning organization is an attractive notion but what happens when things do not turn out as planned? Chapter 5 looks at the contrast between the attractive vision of the learning organization and the more mundane reality of organizational life. Blocks to learning and common learning disabilities, which inhibit or stop us from learning are discussed together with an exploration of the shadow side of the organization.

In one sense all organizations are learning organizations, and one starting point is to look at the learning that happens in the organization at present. Chapter 6 offers some ideas for further developing the learning in your organization. There are ideas about developing organizational learning processes, including the Change Equation, the notion of Organizational Learning Capability and the Organizational Learning Cycle, a case example and ten places to make a start on the learning organization.

Chapter 7 looks at the wider purpose of the learning organization idea. What is all this learning for? Each individual or organization exists in a wider context and needs wider purposes beyond survival and self-interest. The "good company" is one that seeks a "balanced scorecard" meeting the needs of an expanding circle of stakeholders. A case example of Traidcraft shows how one organization does this. Whole systems development is suggested as a way forward for the "good" learning organization.

There are twelve Activities throughout the book designed to apply the learning organization ideas in practice. They have been collected together in Chapter 8 for ease of reference and also to create a resource kit for use with groups and seminars.

SOURCES FOR CHAPTER 1

[1] Holland G. (1986) *Excellence in Industry: Developing Managers – a new approach.* A speech given at Dorchester Hotel, 11 February 1986, Manpower Services Commission, Sheffield.

[2] Pedler, Burgoyne & Boydell (1997) *The Learning Company: A Strategy for Sustainable Development* 2nd Edition, McGraw-Hill, Maidenhead UK, p.3

2. What is the Learning Organization?

IN THIS CHAPTER: The idea of the learning organization is explored. Why has it become part of the vision for so many ambitious enterprises? We argue that the capacity to learn is one of the best guarantors of survival and success in unpredictable times.

Contents

2 What is the Learning Organization?

It sounds familiar. It sounds good, but what does the learning organization actually mean and why should people want to bother with it? Then again, surely it's people who learn, not organizations? This chapter introduces the idea of the learning organization and explains why it is the vision for so many ambitious enterprises. It:

- starts by reviewing the environmental conditions favouring organizations who are skilled at learning

- argues that the capacity to learn might be the best guarantor of survival and success in unpredictable times

- explores the benefits of thinking of organizations as living organisms

- gives several definitions of the learning organization and an opportunity to generate one to suit your own organization

The learning organization arrives

Learning is the new organizational frontier. Our definition of "learning" includes innovation: indeed what is learning if it doesn't lead to a person or an organization seeing, thinking and *doing* differently? Where once quality and excellence were the limits of corporate ambition, the learning organization seeks sustainable performance and development through being flexible, adaptive and responsive to change.

Organizational leaders face one overriding challenge today: how to learn quickly and continuously enough to cope with turbulent and rapidly changing times. Managing change and learning is the No. 1 task; and this applies as much to schools, hospitals and cities as to business and commerce. Developing the learning capacity of the organization is the way ahead.

For commercial enterprises, the learning organization is a major source of sustainable advantage:

> "...learning has become the key developable and tradable commodity of an organization"[1]

In the long run, this learning, and the knowledge and know-how which accrue, is the only thing which a business has to sell, trade, exchange or offer.

Public service organizations such as schools, health organizations, local authorities, the police, armed forces and the emergency services supply the indispensable basis for a civilised society. Yet the pressure to learn and respond to changing needs, demands and circumstances is even greater here than it is in the private sector. The economy may be growing but the welfare state is shrinking, and the "grateful generation" which saw it set up is being replaced by far choosier "consumers". If the public services don't change themselves they will be changed through such means as privatisation, outsourcing, competitive tendering, local management of schools and "best value" contracts.

Voluntary organizations and the not-for-profit sector are equally experiencing difficult and challenging times. Some attempt to shoulder the burden of declining public service provision, whilst others spring up in response to new needs almost daily. Frequently faced with overwhelming demands for their services, the shrinking welfare state is a threat and also sometimes an opportunity to develop new work. Raising funds has become a highly competitive business and traditional methods look increasingly inadequate. New skills of tendering, contracting, selling, public relations and, indeed, managing and organizing rather than administering, are required.

But there is another purpose, beyond survival in their own sectors, for all these organizations to change and learn. Ultimately they all contribute and make a difference to the communities and wider society of which they are part. Perhaps a society gets the sort of organizations it deserves; certainly in a world dominated by organizations of all kinds, it is the quality of these that flavours the nature of that society. Businesses may be ruthless and rapacious or sustaining and socially responsible; public services may be bureaucratic and corrupt or caring and committed to progressive social change; voluntaries may be incompetent and divided or efficient, effective and life-enhancing. Everyone has a stake in the health of these enterprises; good organizations go to make up the good society.

Forces for change and development in organizations

Some major drivers behind the forces for change and learning are set out in the diagram on p.10.[2]

Such pressures reveal the limitations of bureaucratic or autocratic management styles:

> "The old bureaucratic command-and-control model, even in its current decentralised, supposedly lean and mean version, won't be up to the challenges ahead: it won't be fast enough... keen enough... smart and sensitive enough... (we) need a new kind of organization that accommodates radical change, indeed that builds in the capacity to thrive on change."[3]

Is your organization smart and sensitive enough?

Major drivers behind the forces for change and learning

why?

- Fewer people
- Failure of previous re-structurings
- Need to change the culture – How do we do things here?
- Wish to become more people-orientated: Staff and customers
- Link resources more closely with customer needs
- Improve corporate image
- Competitive pressures – need to compete, survive and grow
- Increasing pace of change
- Wish to encourage more active experimentation
- Need to improve quality

Staying afloat

Peter Senge has pointed out that the life expectancy of the average US corporation is less than 40 years.[4] The chances are that, in your working life, you may well experience something like this:

early days

the rise of management

contradiction

confusion

the END

Reg Revans is an architect of this new consciousness, his ecological formula:

$$\mathbf{L \geq C}$$

...holds that the learning in the organization must be equal to or greater than the rate of environmental change[5]. If the learning rate inside is *less* than the rate of external change, then the organization is declining or dying. With all organizations facing rapid and unpredictable changes, this truth has become increasingly obvious; as change accelerates so "organizational death" comes in many guises through failure, acquisition, merger:

> "Of the corporations in the Fortune 500 rankings five years ago, 143 are missing today. (By comparison, in the twenty five years, 1955 to 1980, only 238 dropped out.)".[6]

And again this does not apply only to the commercial sector; public sector organizations are increasingly vulnerable to social and demographic changes and to radical Government policies.

So what makes organizations more likely to survive? De Geus suggests that all the long-lived organizations in his small sample had, in the past, undergone fundamental transformations or "historic organizational learning." They also tended to be:

- financially conservative

- environmentally sensitive

- held together by a strong sense of corporate identity

- able to anticipate change

- tolerant of "experiments at the margin"[7]

These characteristics of "the living company" amount to a fundamental shift in the way we look at organizations. Where we have tended to see them as inanimate machines, we now view them as living organisms. From this perspective, organizations never arrive at a final state but are always in a dynamic process of becoming.

Living organizations

If they are living, then organizations have a *biography* with a birth, stages of development to maturity and finally, a death. Organizations are formed by three forces:

- *Ideas* – the visions and images that founders seek to realise and which are passed on to succeeding generations to re-create;

- *Phase* – the life stage of the company e.g. infant, pioneer, rational, overripe bureaucracy, dying;

- *Era* – the economic, technological, social, political and cultural context.[8]

As already noted the *Era* is one of competitiveness and unprecedented change. *Ideas* are the major source of an organization's difference and "personality". Even when they are in the same business, organizations are built upon different core ideas and purposes. For example, although the two may share some purposes in common, an Oxford college conceives of itself differently from a new university. The *Idea* of the learning organization is one to be interpreted and realised uniquely in each different situation.

Another difference between organizations is their *Phase* of development. Organizations are commonly referred to as people – strong or weak, young or old, informal or cold. In planning how to become a learning organization it helps to think about your organization as a person with its own individual needs for development.

What *Phase* or point has your organization reached in its life cycle? What does it need to do to reach the next stage?

It would be useful to reflect at this point how these ideas apply to your company or organization. On page 120 you will find Activity 1 (Ages and Stages). This invites you to think through your organization's biography with a view to considering what comes next. (Note that there are 12 of these Activities throughout the book, each designed to apply the learning organization ideas in practice. To avoid interrupting the flow of the text, the Activities have been collected together in Chapter 8. A "button arrow" in the text, as shown below, marks each Activity and where it can be found.)

What is a learning organization?

A vision which demands fresh interpretation by each unique organization has many definitions. Senge, whose book *The Fifth Discipline* has been a bestseller on both sides of the Atlantic, describes the learning organization as a place:

> "…where people continually expand their capacity to create the results they truly desire… where people are continually learning how to learn together… where people are continually discovering how they create reality. And how they can change it."[9]

This sounds good – people are learning, changing things and achieving results, but it doesn't give a picture for what actually happens. Karen Watkins and Victoria Marsick are more specific; in such an organization…

> "Learning takes place in individuals, teams, the organization, and even in the communities with which the organization interacts… (it)… is a continuous, strategically used process – integrated with, and running parallel to, work… (which)… enhances organizational capacity for innovation and growth. The learning organization has embedded systems to capture and share learning."[10]

Here learning is of strategic value, it is collected and distributed, designed into work processes and informs all business dealings and transactions. A shorter, more elegant definition comes from *The Learning Company*, written by one of us with our colleagues John Burgoyne and Tom Boydell. The old idea of "company" for any group of people engaged in a joint enterprise, public or private is defined. The learning company is:

> "…an organization that facilitates the learning of all its members and consciously transforms itself and its context."[11]

This definition of two halves is firstly for developing the potential of everyone in the organization, and not just a few senior managers or "high flyers"; and secondly about the self-development of the organization as an organism, including the integration of each individual's learning with that of the company as a whole. The first of these is not so difficult, given the resources and the will, because the methods and technologies exist for encouraging all staff to continuously learn and develop. The process of transforming the organization as a whole organism is more mysterious and challenging, especially when it also includes the wider context and environment.

By adding a new element of stakeholder satisfaction, Nancy Dixon is of great help in this respect, providing clues to the direction of travel. A learning organization makes:

> " intentional use of learning processes at the individual, group and system level to continuously transform the organization in a direction that is increasingly satisfying to stakeholders."[12]

Learning is not simply for organizational survival and success, but for enriching *all* the stakeholders of the enterprise – users, customers, staff, business partners, communities, government and society.

These are just some of the definitions that we like. At this point you might like to think about which of these best fits the aspirations of the people in your organization. Perhaps you have a different way of looking at things? As there is no blueprint, the vision and the reality of the learning organization are developed from within.

You will find a process for creating a definition to suit your situation in the next exercise. Turn now to:

ACTIVITY 2 Page 124

With a vision in sight, you can make a start on bringing it about and looking for ways of enhancing learning for individuals and for the organization as a whole. An example of a printing company with a very particular vision is given on the next page.

CASE STUDY

Keatings – one vision of the learning organization

Keatings of Mold in north Wales is a small but rapidly expanding specialist printer producing high quality packaging for household-name clients such as Cadbury's and Marks & Spencer. Having previously been the managing director of a much larger printing company, Mike Keating was determined not to make the mistakes he saw in action there. Because of his experiences he was resolved not to have managers, trade unions, wage differentials or to let any plant get much bigger than 50 staff.

Curiously it was these "noxiants" which Keatings wanted to avoid which first began to define the learning organization vision for the company. For example, it was the view that everyone should be paid the same high flat rate of pay and that there should be no designated managers apart from Mike and his co-director, Phil. Some of the other elements of the vision were:

- all people to have a picture in their minds of how our business should work – even when it doesn't

- we should always know what others are doing in the industry – worldwide

- learning is part of what everyone is paid for

- it feels as if everyone is responsible for their own business

- everyone should talk to the customers when necessary

- "mutual adjustment meetings" are a normal part of

working through conflicts

- there is more humility and less arrogance between departments

....

Conclusion

Pursuing the vision of the learning organization means that the enterprise is taking learning seriously and putting it at the centre of its values and operating processes. Such an organization makes *intentional* use of the learning:

- of individual people

- of teams, groups and units

- across functional boundaries, between departments and through status levels

- within the whole organization, and

- with the organization's trading partners and stake-holders

You can learn from what others are doing, and you can develop a plan, but it must to some extent be invented to fit the unique mix of people, products, processes, history, aspirations and culture of your company. The learning organization is more of a journey than a destination; best thought of as a star to steer by whilst plotting your own course. Whilst there is room for rational project management, there is just as much for imagination, creativity and risk-taking. Whatever the current situation the answer is the same: weigh up the situation, get quickly into action, and learn from what happens. It is how you do it that counts.

SOURCES FOR CHAPTER 2

[1] Garratt R (1987) *The Learning Organization* Fontana, London p10

[2] Pedler MJ, Burgoyne JG & Boydell TH (1997) *The Learning Company : A Strategy for Sustainable Development* 2nd. Edition McGraw-Hill, Maidenhead, UK p10

[3] Kiechel W (1990) "The Organization that Learns" *Fortune* March 12 pp 75-77

[4] Senge P (1990) *The Fifth Discipline : The Art and Practice of the Learning Organization* Doubleday Currency, New York p17

[5] Revans RW (1998) *The ABC of Action Learning* Lemos & Crane, London

[6] Pascale R T (1991) *Managing on the Edge* Penguin, Harmondsworth, Middx. UK pp11-17

[7] De Geus A (1997) *The Living Company* Nicholas Brealey, London

[8] Pedler, Burgoyne & Boydell (1997) p6/7

[9] Senge P (1990) p3 & 13

[10] Watkins KE & Marsick VJ (1993) *Sculpting the Learning* Organization: Lessons in the Art & Science of Systemic Change Jossey Bass, San Francisco p8/9

[11] Pedler, Burgoyne & Boydell (1997) p3

[12] Dixon N (1994) *The Organizational Learning Cycle : How We Can Learn Collectively* McGraw-Hill, Maidenhead UK p5

3. What Does a Learning Organization Look Like?

IN THIS CHAPTER: In answer to this question, the essential characteristics of the learning organization are set out and examples given of organizations seeking to attain this vision.

Contents

3 What Does a Learning Organization Look Like?

It is possible to get a sense of what the learning organization looks like. In this chapter there are:

- four glimpses or short cases of organizations seeking to attain this vision

- the 11 characteristics of the learning company – a framework for developing the learning organization

- a questionnaire based on the 11 characteristics which can be used to measure how your organization matches up and what could be done to improve it.

Valuing learning

Like people, organizations can get set in their ways. When this happens it may take a shock or a crisis to shake them up to the point where they decide to take a good look at the situation and make changes. Take the UK's Rover Cars for example:

CASE STUDY

Rover

The car maker Rover Group has a history studded with famous names – Austin, Morris and MG – for example. Yet by the 1980s a new direction was needed. As a smaller company in a global market dominated by giants, it would soon disappear if it did not change. A collaboration with Honda of Japan was a radical step and challenged many of the assumptions of the Rover people. But it stemmed, as the then managing director said, from a critical need to learn:

> "As a company we desperately needed to learn.
> We thought there was only one way to run a car manufacturing plant. Our collaboration with Honda taught us differently."

To help with the learning, Rover established the Rover Learning Business, a business within a business, to provide learning and development opportunities to all employees. The message is that everyone needs to be up to date and to keep on developing, and also that the company supports the learning of all employees, and not just a few "high flyers". Everyone is entitled to a Personal Development Budget to follow a Personal Development Plan agreed with their manager, and increasing numbers of people are taking up this offer. Learning has become an important part of company image and the activities of the Rover Learning Business are widely published both inside and outside the company.

•••

This major shock to the system, and the transformation that was eventually achieved, paved the way for Rover's later merger with BMW of Germany.[1]

The learning organization puts learning at the heart of its

enterprise. Rover set out to get everyone involved in the learning business in order to support the changes which needed to happen. However, learning requires trust in others, when we are learning we are open and vulnerable, easily fooled or misled if our teachers are not acting in good faith.

One litmus test for a learning organization is how it deals with mistakes; does it suddenly drop the learning rhetoric and punish or crush people, or does it really live up to its values? Another test is: are the leaders of the organization themselves learning new things? Or is it just personal development for others? At Woodmill School the head teacher put learning at the heart of her practice and tried to demonstrate learning values in her relations with staff.

CASE STUDY

The learning school

Do good teachers first have to be good learners? Woodmill was an old-fashioned school – the teachers respected each other's space and didn't talk about work in the staffroom, sticking to safe topics like homes and holidays. New teachers found it a tough school to learn in – if they asked for help, they were likely to be told, "We had to learn how to teach for ourselves!". They rarely stayed longer than their probationary year if they could help it.

The new head teacher, Mrs Oakley, brought in one or two new staff, and also some new ways of behaving. Although this would be her last school before retirement, she was currently following an Open University course in the teaching of reading to young children. One day she burst excitedly into the staffroom to say, "I've just discovered this research which shows that children naturally look at each page of a book as a whole picture and not as lines of print. This habit is hard to break and that is why it takes so long for them to learn to follow each line along from left to right. It's obvious when you think about it, but how could I have been teaching all these years without realizing that?"

Whilst deprecating herself for not knowing such an "obvious" thing, Mrs Oakley was not embarrassed, it was all part of her enthusiasm for learning. This was typical of her and gradually she introduced a new atmosphere into the school. However, some teachers did not like her new ways and thought that she did not behave "properly". In particular, one senior teacher consistently sought to undermine her efforts.

Three behaviours were central to Mrs Oakley's leadership of learning:

- Be a learner yourself

- Share and demonstrate your new learning

- Persist in confirming learning as a central value, make it normal, and encourage others to do it.

••

Putting learning at the centre includes upholding each person's human rights – to learn at their own pace, to disagree with the direction of change, and the right not to learn or change against their will – this is clearly no soft option for leaders. When organizations are going through periods of rapid change and development these rights are often hard to uphold and any decision not to learn is likely to carry certain consequences. In the Woodmill school case the senior teacher eventually left.

As well as making learning a central value, leading the learning organization demands lots of competences including those of being able to admit ignorance and the occasional ability to "make a fool of yourself" in trying to learn something new.

Given the necessary courage and humility, this can be done in a smallish company of learners like a school, but what about the large multi-national?

CASE STUDY

The networked learning organization

The electrical engineer ABB was created in 1987 by a Swedish/Swiss merger to transform two national institutions into a new kind of company able to operate successfully worldwide.

ABB set out to decentralise radically whilst still operating globally. Recognising that its 200,000 people were mainly committed to their local companies, these were made into 1,200 separate legal and trading entities, with a further sub-division into 4,500 profit centres, each with an average of only 45 people.

How do you hold a radically decentralised organization together? At ABB strong, centralised reporting goes hand in hand with local autonomy. "Abacus", a monthly reporting system, provides performance data on all profit centres which is instantly communicated by electronic data interchange. Other powerful structures and processes link the units together in various networks, including the "Global Networking Hubs" where managers link by business area and country. Great efforts are made to communicate through overlapping information systems.

Promoting continuous exchange of learning is a core value and each ABB company is expected to learn both from elsewhere in the group and to make contributions to the learning of other units. Because of the widely available reporting data, benchmarking within business areas is easy and it is the job of both business area leaders and country CEO's to facilitate learning between companies.

Part of this work is to do with the minimisation of cultural barriers. Chief Executive Percy Barnevik has noted that European managers in particular tend to be selective about sharing information. There is plenty to do in combating such habits in order to realise the vision of speeding and facilitating communication and learning in ABB.[2]

··

Even huge companies can aspire to be learning organizations by seeking to maximise local knowledge whilst minimising parochialism, holding themselves together with a common culture of networking which encourages learning and communication as the "corporate glue".

These "glimpses" of three organizations show them all seeking to maximise both individual and corporate learning as a vital part of carrying out their business and fulfilling their purpose. What else do they have in common beyond making learning a central value?

The 11 characteristics of the learning organization

Those seeking to become learning organizations tend to share some common characteristics. Pedler, Burgoyne and Boydell have suggested a model of the eleven characteristics of the learning organization:[3]

A learning approach to strategy
Where policy and strategy formation are consciously structured for learning purposes – for example, deliberate pilots and small-scale experiments are used to create feedback loops for learning about direction and the creation of "emergent strategy".

Participative policy making

Where all or most members of the organization have a chance to contribute and participate to policy making. Ideally, they do this together with other key stakeholders so that policy reflects and supports a diversity of ideas. This was an aspect of Mrs Oakley's style at Woodmill School that some staff found hard to accept.

"Informating"

In the learning organization information technology is not just about automation but is used to inform people about critical aspects of the business in order to encourage and empower them to act on their own initiative.

Formative accounting and control

This is a particular aspect of "informating" where systems of budgeting, reporting and accounting are structured to assist learning for all members about how money works in the organization.

Internal exchange

Where there is a high degree of internal exchange, as in the ABB case study, learning from other departments is normal and all internal units and departments tend to see themselves as fellow learners in a network, and as customers and suppliers in a supply chain to the end user.

Reward flexibility

Greater autonomy and empowerment for staff leads to a need for more flexible rewards. Here there is flexibility in both monetary and non-monetary rewards to cater for individual needs and performance.

Enabling structures

A wide concept covering not only networked organizational structures – like ABB's – but also including many other aspects of roles, processes and procedures seen as temporary structures, easily changed to meet job or customer requirements.

Boundary workers as environmental scanners

Environmental scanning is carried out by people who have contacts with the outside world of users, suppliers, business partners, neighbours and so on. Processes for bringing back and disseminating information in the organization are also important.

Inter-company learning

As again clearly demonstrated by ABB, the organization meets with others for mutual exchange and learning through benchmarking, joint ventures and other alliances.

A learning climate

A primary focus of Mrs Oakley's efforts at Woodmill School – a good learning climate is one where leaders and managers facilitate their own and other people's experimentation and learning from experience, through questioning, feedback and support.

Self-development opportunities for all

The purpose of the Rover Learning Business – making resources and facilities for self-development available to all members of the organization and not just the favoured few.

These eleven characteristics of the Learning Company give a clear picture of the practices which you would expect to see in an aspiring learning organization. Of course this is an "identikit" and not a real company or organization, but it can serve as a useful template against which to make comparisons.

You can use the following Activity to audit your own organization against these eleven characteristics. Now turn to:

ACTIVITY 3 Page 126

A learning organization profile

Answering the questions in Activity 3 will give suggestions about where you start to build the learning in your organization. Any strengths or weaknesses that you identify will be useful preparation. Here is an example of a profile which shows this particular organization having high scores on Characteristics 1, 10 and 11, but very low scores on 2 (Participative Policy Making) and 6 (Reward Flexibility)[4]:

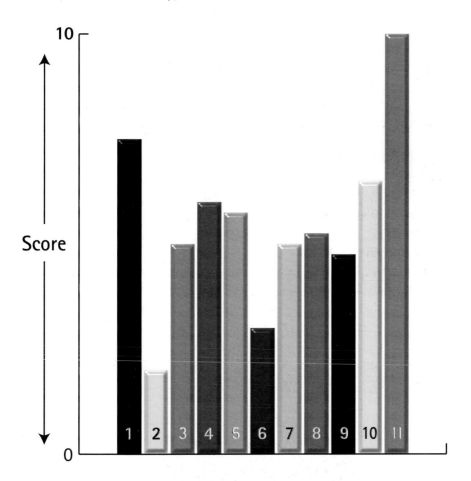

Fig.1 Scores on the 11 characteristics of the learning organization

How would you like it to be?

Do the questionnaire in Activity 3 a second time asking yourself: if this is how it is at the moment, how would I like it to be in future? This second set of scores will provide a "gap analysis", which, in effect, prioritises the Eleven Characteristics of the Learning Company as far as your organization is concerned. From these two scores a *dissatisfaction index* can be calculated:

$$\textit{Dissatisfaction Index} = 100 \text{ x } \frac{\text{How it should be} - \text{How it is}}{\text{How it should be}}$$

If people are totally dissatisfied, this index will be 100. If they are completely satisfied with things as they are, then it is zero. Data from 25 organizations in Fig. 2 shows the rank-order of dissatisfaction in this sample. From this sample the area seen as most in need of strengthening is Participative Policy Making, followed by Reward Flexibility and then Formative Accounting and Control. [5]

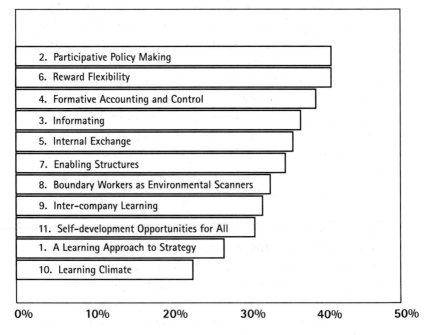

2. Participative Policy Making
6. Reward Flexibility
4. Formative Accounting and Control
3. Informating
5. Internal Exchange
7. Enabling Structures
8. Boundary Workers as Environmental Scanners
9. Inter-company Learning
11. Self-development Opportunities for All
1. A Learning Approach to Strategy
10. Learning Climate

0%   10%   20%   30%   40%   50%

Fig. 2 Dissatisfaction Index – per cent (Sample of 25 organizations)

The short questionnaire in Activity 3 is a useful way of working with a small group of people to stimulate thinking about your organization. However, for an organization-wide survey with a cross-section of various departments and groups, by age, gender, length of service and so on, there are longer, properly validated versions of *The Eleven Characteristics of the Learning Company Questionnaire* in both paper-based and software format.[6]

Once you have done the analysis, what actions are indicated in your particular company? In the case of BICC, below, all eleven characteristics were tackled over a two-year period in a major transformation of this company.

CASE STUDY

BICC Telephone Cables

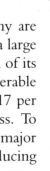

> The eleven characteristics of the learning company are brought to life at BICC Telephone Cables, part of a large UK-based engineering company.[7] The privatisation of its main customer, British Telecom, presented a considerable challenge for BICC with its market share cut to 17 per cent and a healthy profit turned into a major loss. To remain in business BICC Cables had to make major improvements in quality and delivery, whilst reducing price significantly in a shrinking UK market for copper-based cable. In order to respond positively to this threat a two-year organizational development project was created with the help of consultants. This fell into four main phases, which became more apparent in retrospect:
>
> #### Setting the scene
> Lasting for six months, this phase involved the agreement of an overall business strategy, gaining senior management commitment and beginning communications with employees and union representatives. A learning organization strategy was chosen because it was

not a standard blueprint but a process which encouraged "learning through" to BICC's own solution. The company set out to empower people to use their insight and skills, hitherto largely ignored, and integrate individual with organizational development. The learning organization approach was an integrative one, affecting all aspects of the whole and likely to provide the basis for self-sustaining, long-term transformation.

Removing barriers/creating the right environment

Cable manufacturing involves seven sequential processes, each with its own area and with dedicated employees and machinery. Much greater flexibility was needed both within and across these areas. A major hindrance to any form of job flexibility was a cumbersome set of over 30 wage scales and the move to a single, unified wage scale took a long time but was a major change, covering as it did all production employees across all processes and areas. This single-status environment took six months to negotiate and was made more difficult by some redundancies taking place at the same time.

Part of this negotiation was a *People Contract* with *Employer's Undertakings* such as, "stating expectations and setting standards", "listening to employees' views and opinions and providing feedback" and "increasing job-related skills and knowledge and providing further education opportunities" on one side. On the other, there were *Employees' Commitments* such as, "attending regularly and punctually", "operating the required quality system and standards", "providing training to colleagues" and "operating flexibly".

The *People Contract* also contained the *Joint Commitment* "to improve quality, increase productivity, review practices regularly and to respond positively and rapidly to uncertainty".

Introducing teamworking in manufacturing

This phase included the recruitment, selection and training of shift managers, team leaders and their teams. After the training workshops the consultants provided support on the shifts, working with teams and team leaders, facilitating the resolution of issues and using all opportunities for development. Inter-company learning was encouraged with leaders and team members visiting other organizations where teamworking had been established. Information and communications improved generally; the shift managers had met together for the first time ever on the workshops and they now continued to meet fortnightly. In addition, regular meetings were set up with the works manager.

Creating a learning environment

After the basic team training and on-going support was well under way, some further initiatives were taken to promote individual learning and development. An open learning facility was opened on site and a personal development programme for skills such as literacy, numeracy and foreign languages was established. A process improvement initiative was launched and technical skills training was integrated with national qualifications such as NVQs. The company committed itself to gaining the Investors in People award.

Results

Over two years the measurable outcomes of this learning organization effort were impressive. They included reductions in absenteeism and scrap of more than 50 per cent and gains in employee productivity of up to 113 per cent. Helped by new export contracts and better delivery times, UK market share rose from 17 per cent to 40 per cent and the company moved back from loss to profit.

These outcomes were the culmination of many changes over time. By working on all eleven

Characteristics of the Learning Company simultaneously, but not necessarily sequentially, a vessel was created within which people could apply their existing knowledge and acquire new capabilities, not only about how to make cable but also about how to work together.

SOURCES FOR CHAPTER 3

[1] Adapted from Pedler MJ, Burgoyne JG & Boydell TH (1997)
The Learning Company : A strategy for sustainable development
Second Edition McGraw-Hill, Maidenhead pp143/144

[2] Adapted from Pedler, Burgoyne & Boydell (1997) p 93

[3] Pedler, Burgoyne & Boydell (1997) pp 15-18

[4] Pedler, Burgoyne & Boydell (1997) p32

[5] Pedler, Burgoyne & Boydell (1997) p34

[6] Available from the Learning Company Project , 28 Woodholm Rd.,
Sheffield S11 9HT Tel & Fax : 0114 2621832

[7] Pedler, Burgoyne & Boydell (1997) Chapter 19

4. How Can an Organization Learn?

IN THIS CHAPTER: The nature of learning in general and organizational learning in particular.

Contents

4 How Can an Organization Learn?

To answer this question, start with the person. This chapter explores the nature of individual learning and then learning at the organization level. It contains:

- a description of four different kinds or types of learning

- an Activity for thinking about learning at work

- a discussion of what is meant by organizational learning, including Senge's *Five Disciplines of the Learning Organization*

- the Organizational Learning Styles Inventory together with an Activity to apply this to your organization.

Four kinds of learning

Learning is an integral part of what it means to be a human being or, as George Kelly put it, of "getting on with life" . However there is no universally agreed definition of "learning" and people often mean different things when they use the word. One way of putting it is that learning is about *how we change* and become different from the way we were before. Within this simple definition, are four kinds or types:

- Learning *about* things or Knowledge

- Learning to *do* things or Skills, Abilities, Competence

- Learning to *become* ourselves, *to achieve our full potential* or Personal development

- Learning to *achieve things together* or Collaborative enquiry[1].

The first two of these types are the most familiar, used in such pairings as knowledge and skills; theory and practice. Although the split is commonly made, the separation between these two is unhelpful. For example, Business School MBA programmes often teach inexperienced managers "know-that" before they have the necessary "know-how". In contrast, Revans comments about action learning, "There can be no learning without action, and no action without learning."[2]

Personal development involves a person becoming more themself and achieving their full potential. As well as intellect and skill this includes purpose and identity. With this type of learning, there are stages of development, where learning is incremental within stages, but is more of a step-jump or transformation when moving between stages, for example, from being a professional to becoming a manager or from being a "controller" to becoming a "facilitator". The development of the whole person has always been valued by the best teachers but it is now increasingly important in work organizations. This is because of the link between individual personal development and change in the wider system or organization. As Revans has put it:

> "Those unable to change themselves, cannot change what goes on around them."[3]

Linked to this is the fourth type of learning, collaborative enquiry, which although less familiar, is one of the keys to organizational learning. Learning is usually seen as a property of the person; something which individuals do, on their own, happening inside them. Suppose, however, that learning can also take place between people – in the spaces or relationships between them – and that individuals can co-operate in collective learning. Action learning and team learning aim at this – where the outcomes cannot be fully measured in terms of what individuals take away, but by what is created together.

Collaborative enquiry forms a bridge between individual learning and the learning organization. Understanding it better will help in the transforming of organizations as whole systems. Organizations usually focus on individuals – recruiting, selecting, training, appraising, career planning, retiring and sacking them as isolated people. Although it will include all forms of individual learning, the learning organization is ultimately about learning relationships and what goes on between people. Some organizations create better conditions for this sort of learning than others. They make learning a value at the heart of the enterprise, they encourage people to talk to each other, they simply have a better "learning climate".

The first step in considering the development of a good learning climate is to start with yourself and your own learning. How do you learn best? Which factors in yourself and in your immediate environment help you to learn most effectively? And which factors inhibit your learning? You can explore these questions more fully in the next exercise. Turn now to:

ACTIVITY 4 Page 132

In thinking about your own learning, you will have noted some of the common blockages or barriers which stop learning. Young children, given a safe and loving environment, easily soak up knowledge, daily develop new skills, play freely at imitating others and look forward eagerly to being someone else! Grown-ups are more knowledgeable, skillful *and* inhibited, cautious, with much more to give up. Whilst adults are no less in need of a safe and loving environment, they learn best when there is some challenge to their current ways of doing things, as well as the encouragement to learn new ways with and from each other.

For some large organizations it has become something of a fashion to set up company "universities". One of the pioneers of this work, Motorola, has sought to make learning central to the manufacturing process.

CASE STUDY

Motorola U

> Motorola University has its origins in the realisation that quality is increasingly critical as new technologies change the rules of manufacturing under conditions of global competition. The company found that many of its people could not read very well – for example, it is said that only 40 per cent of those in one plant could answer the question, "Ten is what per cent of 100?"
>
> Motorola then launched an ambitious scheme of education and training for its staff, and then extended this not only to all employees worldwide but also to suppliers, principal customers and even to educational providers. The term "university" may seem a little pretentious, but programmes are delivered with the help of a wide range of educational partners who provide resources and validation. The ambition is also there – the focus of training is now for the person as well as for the job, in order to:

> "Create an environment for learning, a continuous openness to new ideas… anticipating new technologies… not only teaching skills (but) trying to breathe the very spiral of creativity and flexibility into manufacturing and management."[4]

Motorola offers one response to the question, "How can an organization learn?", by encouraging everyone to make the "learning habit" a normal part of working life. Many aspiring learning organizations interpret the idea in terms of individual learning opportunities. Although this is a useful step, no amount of individual development alone will produce an organization able to change itself as a whole. The learning organization is not just the training organization:

> "… organizational learning is not the same thing as individual learning, even when the individuals who learn are members of the organization. There are too many cases in which organizations know less than their members. There are even cases in which the organization cannot seem to learn what every member knows."[5]

What is organizational learning?

With a literature reaching back at least to the 1960s, organizational learning is not a new concept, but it is suddenly very popular. The terms "learning organization" and "learning company" are descendants of the "learning system" idea discussed by Revans in 1969[6] and Schon in 1970.[7]

But just how it is that an organization can be said to learn is not immediately obvious. For a start, it calls into question – as in Argyris and Schon's "What is an organization that it may learn?"[8] – what is meant by the word "organization"? Using organic rather than mechanical metaphors for organizations helps here, for whilst machines are inanimate and programmed, organisms are alive and can learn. This makes it possible to think about organizations as living systems or organisms, and thus the idea of learning follows.

Looking at organizations in this way, it is clear that without learning processes taking place on an every day basis, they could not function. You can see organizational learning in action in many different contexts. The link between individual and organizational learning is now a pressing concern. How can it become a natural part of what is meant by "organization"?

Five disciplines for the learning organization

Senge suggests that there are five disciplines to master:

- Personal Mastery

- Sharing Mental Models

- Building Shared Vision

- Team Learning

- Systems Thinking.

Personal Mastery

Personal Mastery is self-development – the discipline of "continually clarifying and deepening our personal vision, of focussing our energies, of developing patience and of seeing reality objectively". This is a life-long process deepening personal aims and purposes and living in a state of continuous learning to become what we may be.

Sharing Mental Models

Albert Einstein said, "Our theories determine what we measure."

Everyone has pre-conceptions and assumptions – their own view of the world. Mental models influence how different people see and do things. People may disagree because they do not understand each other's perceptions of the problem. A learning organization needs to "think collectively" in dialogue and debate so that the diversity of personal and shared constructs of the world are explored. This can help with building Shared Vision.

Shared Vision

A collective picture of the future which fosters "genuine commitment and enrolment rather than compliance". People then "excel and learn, not because they are told to but because they want to".

Team Learning

Some teams really gel so much that it is hard in retrospect to say who thought of what. These are key units of the learning organization. The discipline of Team Learning involves dialogue: the capacity creatively to explore ideas and suspend our own judgments in a free-flow of meaning whereby the team "thinks" as a single organism.

Systems Thinking

This fifth discipline underpins and integrates the others. Systems Thinking is a methodology for seeing in wholes and for recognising the patterns and the interrelatedness of parts which go to make up these wholes. This discipline means working with the patterns, relationships and subtle interconnections of the learning organization as a living system.

However, this is not easy, all too often, "We are literally killing ourselves through being unable to think in wholes"[10]

To what extent are the five disciplines practised in your organization?

Organizational learning styles

Another way to think about this is to consider what sort of learning goes on in an organization. In what ways is the organization good at learning and what is it less good at? Like people, organizations can be said to have various styles of learning. Here are five organizational learning styles that can apply to the organization as a collective, living and learning, system:

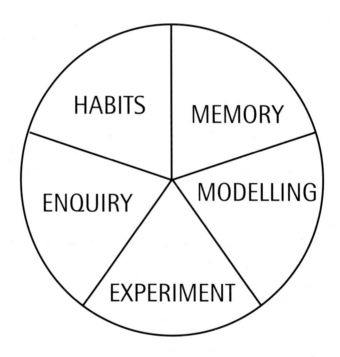

Each of the five organizational learning styles has strengths and, if over-relied upon, significant weaknesses:

Habits
Strength = Good at forming habits and standard operating procedures, which survive the turnover of individuals and are important for long term survival.
Downside = The danger of unthinking repetition after the habit has ceased to be functional – the "Blind Automaton" Syndrome.

Memory

Strength = Good at collecting, storing and disseminating experience, data and knowledge.

Downside = Can be past-oriented, relying on solutions to yesterday's problems – the "Resistance to Change" Syndrome.

Modelling

Strength = Good at imitating, cherry picking and benchmarking best practice internally and externally.

Downside = A danger of over-valuing external ideas leading to lack of belief in our ability to innovate internally – the "Others Lead, We Follow" Syndrome.

Experiment

Strength = Strong on innovation, trial and error, and active experimenting with new ways of doing things.

Downside = The risk of fixing what "ain't broke", of having too many ideas and a preference for experiment over production – the "Flavour of the Month" Syndrome.

Enquiry

Strength = Good at reflecting on experience, being open-minded and curious, with a wide awareness of the organization, its context and environment.

Downside = Too much enquiry can lead to a loss of focus and lack of attention to detail – the "Ivory Tower" Syndrome.

Try the next Activity to see what your organization is good at – and not so good at – and what the consequences of this might be. Turn now to:

ACTIVITY 5 Page 136

The organizational learning styles analysis in Activity 5 can be used in a variety of ways. Styles may vary by unit, department or section. Different groups can choose a particular style in order to become more well-rounded in their approach to learning. For example, a large multi-national company decided to embark on a project to improve "organizational memory" in relation to a particular joint venture because they keep making the same mistake in different parts of the world.

This chapter has looked at what organizational learning means; in the next we look more closely about what can go wrong. What blocks learning in organizations? And what about the "Shadow Side" of the learning organization?

SOURCES FOR CHAPTER 4

[1] Pedler MJ & Aspinwall KA (1996) *"Perfect plc?" : The Purpose and Practice of Organizational Learning* McGraw-Hill, Maidenhead, UK p25

[2] Revans RW (1998) *The ABC of Action Learning* Lemos & Crane, London

[3] Revans RW (1998)

[4] Adapted from Pedler MJ, Burgoyne JG & Boydell TH (1997) *The Learning Company : A Strategy for Sustainable Development* 2nd. Edition McGraw-Hill, Maidenhead, UK p160

[5] Argyris C & Schon D (1978) *Organizational Learning : A theory of action perspective* Addison Wesley, Reading, Mass. p9

[6] Revans RW (1982) "The Enterprise as a Learning System" in *The Origins and Growth of Action Learning* Chartwell Bratt, Bromley, UK pp 280-286

[7] Schon DA (1971) *Beyond the Stable State* Random House, New York

[8] Argyris C & Schon D (1978) Ch 1

[9] Senge P (1990) *The Fifth Discipline : The Art and Practice of the Learning Organization* Doubleday Currency, New York pp 6-16)

[10] Senge P (1991) "The Learning Organization made Plain" *Training & Development* October pp 37-44

[11] Pedler MJ & Aspinwall KA (1996) p94-99

5. What Can Go Wrong?

IN THIS CHAPTER: The contrast between the attractive vision of the learning organization and the mundane reality of organizational life. Blocks to learning and common learning disabilities, which inhibit or stop us from learning are discussed together with an exploration of the shadow side of the organization.

Contents

5 What Can Go Wrong?

So far in this book, we have defined the learning organization, glimpsed a range of possibilities of what it looks like and discussed how organizations can learn as whole organisms. So far, so good – but what happens when things don't turn out as planned? What can go wrong?

The learning organization is but the latest in a long list of ideas and visions which have promised better futures for people in organizations. Scientific management, human relations theory, open systems thinking, organization development, strategic planning, the search for excellence, TQM, BPR and so on all contain good ideas, but usually over-promise and under-deliver. As a child of several of these, why should the learning organization be different?

Unlike many packaged ideas the learning organization has to be realised from within, based on the aims and aspirations of the people concerned. It offers a star to steer by. To use such an idea wisely the downsides or shadows which accompany all powerful visions must be understood together with how these can affect the best efforts. In other words, when starting out bravely on the quest it is as well to know what can go wrong.

This chapter addresses:

- The contrast between the attractive vision of the learning organization and the more mundane and often paradoxical reality of organizational life.

- What blocks learning and diverts learning energy into unhelpful directions – in particular what are the common learning disabilities which inhibit or stop people learning?

- The shadow side of the organization.

The chapter ends with the rather provocative OTI or Organizational Toxicity Index. Before the learning organization can thrive, there may be some preparatory work needed – at the moment, in reality, just how toxic or poisonous is your company?

Getting real

Two conversations with senior managers from large organizations reveal a different reality from the brilliance of the learning organization vision:

"The current reality of my life in my organization is a long long way away from what you're saying. I can see the idea but I can't see how I can get there from where I am now."

"We thought we were a learning company, but now we realise we're not. We are into action, into problem-solving but not into reflection and learning from those problems. In our company it is not easy to admit mistakes. You are not allowed to be weak. We need to be in control all the time. There are lots of denials. Expertise is what counts."

The learning organization idea has been in vogue at least since the publication of Senge's *The Fifth Discipline* in 1990, but there is still a big gap between the idea and the reality as experienced by many people in organizations. It seems that organizations are not always very good at learning:

"Learning disabilities are tragic in children… They are no less tragic in organizations, where they also go largely undetected."[1]

Learning disabilities in organizations

Sometimes problems can be blamed on particular individuals who manifest much the same kind of behaviour no matter where they are or with whom they work. Yet behaviour is often situational with certain conditions bringing out the best or the worst in people. So it is important to think at the level of the whole organization. What influences people? What encourages individuals, teams and departments to learn? And, what stops organizations learning?

The average life span of the US corporation is now as low as 40 years. Today's employee has a fifty-fifty chance of seeing the firm they work for disappear during their working life.[2] As the pace of change increases there are likely to be more stories like the one below.

CASE STUDY

Wang Laboratories

In August 1992, Wang Laboratories, once a $3 billion powerhouse of the computing industry, filed for bankruptcy protection after losses of over $1.5 billion in four years, a victim of the recession and failure to adapt to rapid technological change. The company is planning to shed 5,000 of the remaining 13,000 staff, down from a late 1980s peak of 31,500. Founded in

1951 by Chinese immigrant An Wang, the company pioneered word processing equipment and flourished in the 1970s and early 1980s. But Wang was focussed on mid-sized computers using proprietary systems and was slow to adapt to the advent of personal computers. Poor management by Mr Wang's son and heir Frederick accelerated the decline. A new Chairman was brought in at a salary of $1 million in 1989 and promised a "new Wang"; but, having been previously with General Electric's TV operations, he had no experience of the computer world, and the turnaround did not happen.[3]

In the fast-paced computer business, the real test of a learning organization is not whether it slips or not, but whether it can learn from the inevitable mistakes quickly enough. Though Wang recovered to some extent, the fallout from the *Fortune 500* companies noted in Chapter 1 shows that many do not.

Without actually going to the wall, examples of organizations failing to learn are legion. Argyris describes a study by Beer, Eisenstat and Spector of six large companies which invested heavily in change programmes to change the many poor practices which were rendering the companies ineffective. These poor practices included:

- inflexible and unadaptive rules

- managers and workers out of touch with customer needs

- managers who were not committed, not co-operative and not competent to produce change

- poor interaction amongst functional groups

- top management refusing to believe that lower revenues and market share were more than a temporary perturbation

- lack of strategic thinking

- lower level employees not fully informed

- low levels of trust.[4]

Yet, despite these pressing needs to learn, the authors reported that all the programmes failed, either wholly or partly. They began with a big fanfare but then just faded away. Senge suggests that this is because organizations typically suffer from severe "learning disabilities", described below.

"I Am My Position"
– a narrow focus on *my* job rather than on the purpose of the whole.

"The Enemy Is Out There"
– we blame others when things go wrong, yet "in here" and "out there" are part of the same system.

"The Illusion of Taking Charge"
– "taking charge" is often a reaction response to the "out there"; true pro-activeness comes from seeing how we contribute to our own problems.

"The Fixation On Events"
– a focus on short-term events means that we don't notice the slow gradual processes, such as...

The Parable of the Boiled Frog
– where subtle changes in the environment which are not detected until it is too late, and yet we persist in...

The Delusion of Learning From Experience
– although we learn best from experience, many of our decisions impact mainly on others; we act in isolation and our actions have unintended consequences of which we know nothing.

The Myth of the Management Team
– "teams" may appear cohesive and function well on routines, but they are full of internal "turf" conflicts and can fall apart under pressure. Or as Senge himself puts it:

> "How can a team of committed managers with
> individual IQs above 120 have a collective IQ of 63?"[5]

These learning disabilities are made worse by a reactive stance to change, seen as coming from out there, rather than generating a vision of where the organization wants to be and how it is going to get there. There are three levels of explanation in any system:

Level 1:	Events	Reactive
Level 2:	Patterns of behaviour	Responsive
Level 3:	Systemic structure	Generative[6]

Seeing things as isolated events leads to *reactive* behaviour where other people or groups are blamed for what goes wrong. Understanding events in terms of patterns of behaviour enables organizations and people to avoid the reactiveness trap and become responsive to trends. Systemic structure is the deepest level of explanation, showing what causes the patterns of behaviour where, because of feedback loops and delays, spirals and cycles, it is likely that no one person is to blame, but that the problem is a joint production of many individual actions. This is generative because it provides the deeper insights that enable people to reflect upon their patterns of behaviour and begin to think about how they might change them.

As generative thinking, based on an understanding of the systemic structure, seems to be the best way to go, what stops people doing this sort of "joined-up thinking"?

The organizational Shadow

Explaining why clips from the film *Batman and Robin* should be used in Domestos advertisements, CEO Simon Thong claimed that :

> "Like Batman, Domestos has a slightly menacing and
> dark side to its nature"[7]

There are many different terms for the shadow or hidden side of people and organizations – the informal, dark, hidden, shadow, underside, double, demonic or doppelganger. The Shadow side, balancing the light side, is a very old idea, common in myths, history and religions. It is also a critical aspect of the most cherished writings; Shakespeare's tragedies, for example, tend to be valued more highly than his comedies.

It is used every day to explain common paradoxes in the world. "He means well" they say, indicating, as Dr Deming put it, that people are often "crushed by their own best efforts". Equally familiar are warnings, after Robert Burns, about the likely outcomes of "the best laid plans". When things do go wrong, this may be put down to bad luck or to a mischievous universe, but it may also be a negative reflection of what we really, really wanted to go right!

Yet the Shadow is almost entirely absent from the cheerful literature of business and management. Here the song is "Always Look on the Bright Side of Life" and stones are left unturned. This is a denial of the Shadow, which has two faces, for it is not only an ever-present tripping-up device as manifest in "Sod's Law" but also a source of great power, of extraordinary energy and superhuman performance. When Nietzsche called for a self-development quest to the level of the "Superman" he was seeking to access this power in all people. Great artists – and "great" criminals – release their Shadow energies in pursuit of their goals. Corporate leaders, calling for "110 per cent performance" and prepared to make huge sacrifices in pursuit of being the best, also seek to tap these same energies.

As the power builds, so do the negative energies or "the double". High performing organizations are lionised, but the distressing, shameful or destructive aspects of life in these organizations is not usually noticed. To ignore the Shadow is to risk complacency and the hubris that will eventually follow; yet to engage with it is equally perilous. Faust embraced the Shadow when he sold his soul for earthly power and success and this myth is reflected in plenty of examples from present times. To give all for high performance is to risk being captured or taken over. But knowing all this is not going to stop the push for better performance. Understanding how the Shadow falls on the very best efforts may help to avoid the worst of the traps.

Two faces of the Shadow

A major problem in talking about the Shadow side and its many synonyms is that these terms are used to mean different things. Two common meanings are:

- the *informal or hidden* aspect – which exists beyond the public face of the organization and is not so much good or bad but complementary to formal structures and processes. This can contribute both to effective organizational working and to furthering narrow individual or sectional interests.

- the *demonic or double* aspect – the negative or evil side that may be often an exaggeration, distortion or degeneration of good or positive qualities. The double is encountered when people seek to call up extraordinary energy or performance – as positive power increases, so does the potential for negative outcomes. This is a simple "law", much celebrated in myths, but which seems destined to be easily forgotten and hence always to be replayed.

The Shadow as informal or hidden

Roger Plant[8] uses the metaphor of an iceberg to differentiate between the formal and informal faces of the organization.

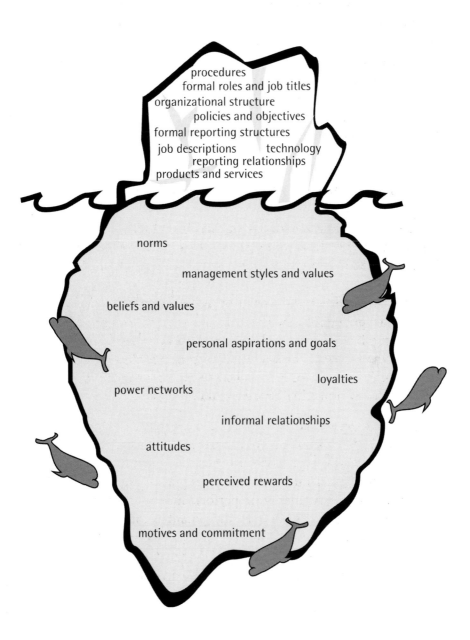

The top of the iceberg is the rational and logical domain into which many managers put their energies and that is well managed. Unless attention is directed equally towards "the submerged, however, murky and often uncharted depths" beneath, little sustainable change will occur.

Change strategies often concentrate on the easily visible formal side of the organization. It also helps to explain why popular activities such as change programmes and "restructurings" often have so little impact after the first phase is over – stress and inconvenience for some and excitement for others. Also it is not always possible to separate neatly the rational and the emotional. Anyone who has been involved in an apparently rational restructuring will know that logic and emotion are often far more difficult to separate than this image implies. As David Casey[9] has said, organizations engage in "the tiring game of pretending that work is an intellectual activity".

The informal aspect of the Shadow is never more obvious when comparing the company rhetoric with people's lived experience. When he read to them the company manual text, "People are our most important asset", Egan[10] reports that a group of employees laughed. When asked how they saw the reality of the situation, they replied:

'People are expendable.'

'You're only as good as yesterday's results.'

'If there's a drop in sales, hide, because you – not the managers – are going to be blamed.'

'Find out what's in your bosses mind and do it.'

'Keep innovative ideas to yourself.'

Egan identifies five aspects of the shadow side present in all organizations:

- organizational culture (which he calls the controlling factor)
- personal styles
- organizational social systems
- organizational politics
- the hidden organization.

Is your organization political? To find out answer the questions below.

Are there people and groups inside your organization who....

... enjoy the use of power?   Yes ☐ No ☐

... vie for scarce resources?   Yes ☐ No ☐

... protect their own "turf"?   Yes ☐ No ☐

... have different ideologies and values?   Yes ☐ No ☐

... compete with others to "win" battles?   Yes ☐ No ☐

Five "Yesses" and you are part of a normal organization!

All organizations are political. Politics can work to enhance or to damage organizational effectiveness; whether they are good or bad depends upon your particular viewpoint and interest. Political activity clearly impacts on the organization's ability to learn and will affect any learning organization strategy. For example, how would you predict that Egan's employees would react if their company announced it was to become a learning organization?

The informal, political organization is familiar and relatively easy to spot in practice. However there is another meaning of the idea of the Shadow; a different, more scary, explanation for why things do not turn out as planned.

The Shadow as double or demonic

This ever-present aspect of development can be illustrated by looking at the evolution of ideas about organizations. Any good idea either fades over time or becomes stronger but somehow distorted, the result of too much of a good thing. Thus *excellence* can degenerate into complacency, and the order and structure of *bureaucracy* – Max Weber's ideal organizational model – can become rigid and compartmentalised. These "doubles" or distorted forms of what was originally good, mirror the forces of disorder and decay found in the physical world.

Though the emergence of the double is destructive, it also has, however, a creative, revitalising role. When the double gets the upper hand, we are on the threshold for the next developmental step, for the next new good idea. One of us with our colleagues suggest that the learning organization emerges from a series of good ideas, each of which fades or becomes distorted and gives way in turn to a new good idea. This is illustrated in Fig. 3 on p.67. Without the "problem" of the old idea, the new "solution" cannot emerge.[11]

As one problem is solved so another eventually emerges, the seeds of which were sown by the way the earlier problem was solved. So S3 will soon lead to P4. This "law of development" explains why the learning organization – or indeed any other vision – never finally arrives.

In turning from ideas to people and organizations the double or demonic takes on a more tragic and heroic form. Mortals seem most in danger when they espouse high ideals – how much evil as well as good has been done in the name of God and Country? Harrison notes the demonic side of so-called excellent or high performing organizations:

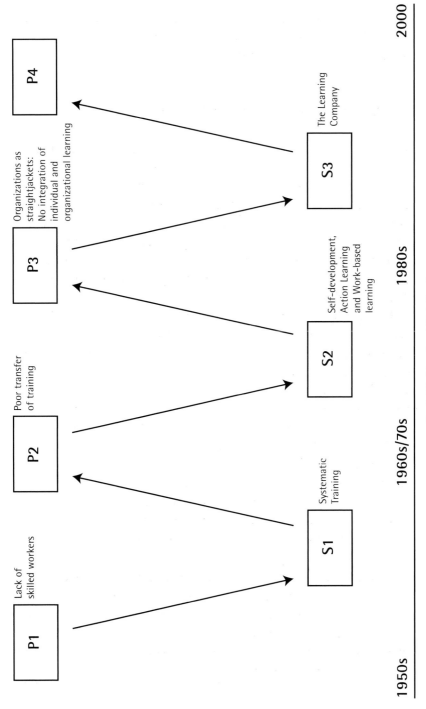

Fig. 3 "Problems" and "Solutions"

"... high performing organizations have their inhumanities. They burn people out; they take over people's private lives; they ostracise or expel those who do not share their purposes; and they are frequently ruthless in their dealings with those outside the magic circle : competitors, suppliers, the public. It seems to me no accident that many of our most exciting tales of high-performing, closely aligned organizations are either literally or metaphorically "war stories". War is the ultimate expression of unbridled will in the pursuit of noble ends."[12]

Burrell takes this even further in his often excruciating journey through the underside of organizational life and theory. He argues that the significance of Taylorism was not so much the "scientific management" of skilled labour but a system for processing European peasant immigrants who had only worked the land, who usually had no English, into effective factory workers. Proclaiming that "Linearity Kills" he further suggests that this genius for organising and processing people from one state to another has its truly demonic outcome in the killing fields of the First World War and the gas chambers of Auschwitz.

"Originally the Nazi plan had been to put Jewish individuals in Madagascar or east of a line drawn between the Asian cities of Archangel and Astrakan. But extermination was decided upon on cost grounds from 21 October 1941 and the classic Weberian elements of precision, speed, unambiguity, knowledge of the files, continuity, discretion, unity, strict subordination, reduction of time, reduction of material and in any 'personal' elements were all put into place to achieve this goal. [13]

If this is truly too awful to dwell upon, a speedy return to the business world of the present day reveals, with some irony, a company that has already appeared in this book as a glimpse of what the learning organization might look like. Commenting on the current trend to "downsizing", Burrell reports Tom Peters quoting a speech by the Chief Executive Officer of ABB.

> "... he commented that during the first year of Asea's owning Brown Boveri they had managed to modestly trim the corporate staff of Brown Boveri back from its prior 4,000 people down to 100. Now some of you snicker when I say that, some of you weep. Some of you become ill at your stomach. All three responses are appropriate. My simple comment, whether you are a middle manager, whether you are a chief executive officer, is if you look at that number and think it is amusing, you do not understand what is going on around you."[14]

Linearity kills. The demonic emerges from any good idea taken too far. In his marvellous book on the Hopi, "an intensely religious people, a confirmed people of peace, with an inherent repulsion against secular control of any kind",[15] Frank Waters re-tells, in one of the key myths, how the Spider Woman warned the Hopi against too much of a good thing:

> "The land was long, wide and beautiful. The earth was rich and flat, covered with trees and plants, seed-bearers and nut-bearers, providing lots of food. The people were happy and kept staying there year after year. 'No. This is not the Fourth World', Spider Woman kept telling them. 'It is too easy and pleasant for you to live on, and you would soon fall into evil ways again. You must go on. Have we not told you the way becomes harder and harder". [16]

So there you have it. The learning organization is a very good thing indeed – but the path is not straight, you never arrive there and if you persist it gets harder! People sometimes make it harder for themselves by setting up ambitious visions and pushing to achieve them. Push and drive are important but they also feed the demonic.

How healthy is your organization?

The vision of a learning organization is of a healthy, beautiful place; fit for human beings to live and learn in. Yet many of today's organizations are less than healthy, and some are downright toxic.

To check the toxicity of your organization turn now to:

Hopefully your results will be strengthening rather than depressing. Whatever the score it is interesting to ask where these characteristics of the organization come from. In a toxic organization the search will no doubt be for someone to blame, but an organization seeking to learn will pose different questions, asking, "What part does each of us play in this process? What does this team contribute? What can be done to change the situation?"

Like any organism, the learning organization thrives best in a healthy ecology. You could do worse in making a start than thinking about how you could clean up the toxicity in the organization, rather than building airy, exotic visions that may blind.

CASE STUDY

Middlewich Hospital

At Middlewich Hospital Trust morale was low and sickness rates amongst staff were high. This led to all sorts of daily difficulties made worse by a general working climate of unwillingness to be flexible and responsive. It was easy for all parties to blame the others. Managers blamed the workforce, the workforce blamed the managers and both groups blamed the Health Authority and/or the Government. Then the situation changed. Some key newly appointed managers were able to avoid the knee-jerk responses to this negative atmosphere – such as increasing supervision, control and punishment, as happens in so many organizations. They began demonstrating trust in their staff. People were told that, if they had an important reason for taking any time out during work such as a dental appointment, they no longer had to use their holiday time to do this. Once the initial surprise was over staff began to respond in kind. Sickness rates fell, work rates and general goodwill increased. The organization became more flexible and responsive to the needs of working parents and those who cared for elderly parents. Trust began to replace blame in this particular culture.

SOURCES FOR CHAPTER 5

[1] Senge P (1990) *The Fifth Discipline : The Art and Practice of the Learning Organization* Doubleday Currency, New York p 18

[2] Senge (1990) p 9

[3] *Source:* Articles by Mark Tran, *The Guardian* (London) 18 and 19 August 1992

[4] Argyris C (1990) *Overcoming Organizational Defences : Facilitating Organizational Learning* Allyn & Bacon, Boston p 3/4

[5] Senge (1990) p 18-25 & p9

[6] Senge (1990) p 52

[7] *The Guardian* 4 April 1997

[8] Plant R (1987) *Managing Change and Making It Stick* Fontana, London

[9] Casey D (1993) *Learning in Organizations* Open University Press, Buckingham UK p43

[10] Egan G (1994) *Managing the Shadow Side* Jossey Bass, San Francisco p9

[11] Pedler MJ, Burgoyne JG & Boydell TH (1997) *The Learning Company : A Strategy for Sustainable Development* Second Edition McGraw-Hill, Maidenhead UK p12-14

[12] Harrison R (1995) *The Collected Papers of Roger Harrison* McGraw-Hill, Maidenhead UK p169

[13] Burrell G (1997) *Pandemonium* Sage, London p141/142

[14] Burrell (1997) p172

[15] Waters F (1977) *The Book of the Hopi* Penguin, Harmondsworth, UK p120

[16] Waters (1977) p19

6. Creating the Learning Organization

IN THIS CHAPTER: In one sense all organizations are learning organizations, and one starting point is to look at the learning that happens in the organization at present. This chapter gives ideas for further developing the learning in your organization.

Contents

6 Creating the Learning Organization

"I hear a lot of talk about the learning organization
these days. I can see why it might be a good idea, but
how do you do it?"

This manager's comment is typical. The excitement about
learning organizations is not yet matched by much solid
experience or examples of how to go about it.

However, in one sense all organizations are learning
organizations: any existing business or institution must, at a
minimum, have learned enough to survive. So, rather than
belabouring yourselves for not being a learning organization, look
at the learning that happens in the organization at present:

- What sort of learning is happening in your
  organization? For example,

    What do we consistently get right?

    What are we good at picking up quickly?

    What new ideas and methods should we be
    considering?

- Who is learning about what? For example,

    Who are the learners around here?

    Who do we go to for advice and guidance?

    Where are the innovative "hot spots" in the
    organization?

- As a whole company, what are we learning from the actions we are taking? For example,

  > How many experiments do we have running on the side?

  > When did we last meet together to discuss the business?

  > What lessons have emerged in the last year or so?

Chapter 6 offers some ideas for further developing the learning in your organization. It contains:

- an Activity to check your organizational readiness to learn

- ten places to make a start on the learning organization

- ideas about developing organizational learning processes including the Change Equation and the notion of Organizational Learning Capability

- an Activity to help you think about how things get done in your organization (and therefore how they might be changed) by mapping your Organizational Learning Cycle

- and a case example of an organization that is gaining advantage from its learning processes through combining the ability to experiment with the ability to "stick to the knitting".

First of all, how ready are you – as an organization – to learn? This will depend on the learning that has been done so far, and what sort of learning that has been.

Activity 7 takes a spot check on your organizational readiness to learn. Now turn to:

ACTIVITY 7 Page 144

As noted in earlier chapters, those organizations that set out deliberately to encourage individual and organizational learning share some common positive characteristics. Alongside these commonalities however are all sorts of ways in which each organization is unique in its history, products, people, ambitions, culture and ideas. Any resemblance between them stems from a desire to encourage learning, but their visions of themselves as organizations that can learn are always unique as are their ways of getting there.

Start here

Transformation often comes from a re-arrangement or alteration of what already exists. If organizations resemble organisms, then each small part – every department or section – has some capacity to affect the whole. When learning breaks out in one part it has the potential to affect the others. Though the "learning department" might flourish best in the "learning company" (which might flourish best in the "learning society"), it has to start somewhere. You can start moving on anywhere that seems possible and appropriate.

Here are ten different starting points for developing your learning organization strategy[1]. They are not mutually exclusive and you can follow more than one or even all of these. Start where the energy is: Who is keen and interested? Where are the hot spots? If none of these quite fits, what does?

The Board

This is the obvious place to start because sooner or later they will have to support the idea if it is to spread. If the directors practice the principles and demonstrate their learning with those with whom they come into contact, the effect will be powerful. Revans puts this at the top of his list of conditions for the learning organization:

> "that its chief executive places high amongst his own responsibilities that for developing the enterprise as a learning system; this he will achieve through his personal relations with his immediate subordinates, since the conduct of one level of a system towards any level below it is powerfully influenced by the perception that the higher level has of its own treatment from above ..."[2]

Diagnosis

Data collection and feedback is a way of raising awareness and starting a dialogue. You could use the Eleven Characteristics of the Learning Organization Questionnaire from Activity 3. To avoid paralysis by analysis (some people prefer gathering data to getting on and doing something) the best approach is action research or action learning, which includes data gathering as part of taking action and learning.

A "Big Event"

A Whole Systems Development approach (described in the next chapter) aims to "get everyone in the room at the same time". When everyone who is "part of the problem" is also part of the change process, a huge quantity of new ideas, energy and commitment is generated. The lack of open debate in some organizations makes this a testing time for leaders or directors who will need help to prepare themselves for "public learning" forums. To avoid later disillusionment energy-raising activities such as these need persistent follow-through.

A Consciousness-raising Development Programme

Organizations seeking to "change the way we do things around here" often use large-scale campaigns to get their message across, including training programmes for all staff such as "Putting People First" or "Quality means getting it right first time". However, as we have already noted, many stand-alone cultural change efforts do not work and must be carefully prepared for *and* backed up by a sustained development strategy to honour the high energy and expectations generated.

A Joint Union/Management Initiative

Any alliance of adversaries has great developmental potential because of the opportunities to challenge and transform old assumptions and methods of working. True dialogue requires differences to help break up existing mental models, patterns and positions. If the conditions exist for this in your organization, and you are up to it, this is a good one to go for. Not for the faint-hearted.

Task forces

Possibly a safer alternative, task forces can look at any dimensions of the learning organization that you wish to pursue. Like action learning groups they work best with sponsors to whom they are accountable. As temporary structures, they will not threaten senior people too much – although unless they pose some sort of threat and meet some resistance they will also not succeed in changing anything. They can mobilize large amounts of energy and creativity, but this can be easily squandered by uncommitted sponsors.

The Strategic Planning Cycle

Another good place to start, if you have one, because it is at the heart of thinking about the future of the organization. The planning cycle can itself be a learning process especially if you build in feedback loops and opportunities for people to have a say and make a contribution to future directions.

Major Priority for Change

If you could wave a magic wand and change just one thing about your organization what would it be? Well, now we have got the fantasies out of the way, what is the single most important priority for change? When change happens it is rarely designed to help people learn about the new situation or conditions. In fact changes are often made in a *non*-learning manner: quickly imposed with little consultation with those affected, without time for trial and error, reflection and learning. How could you design the change process consciously as a learning process?

A Hot Spot

If there is the energy and vision in a particular work group or section then start here. Innovation can happen in unpredictable places. Supposing the Finance Department became interested in "stakeholder accounting"; why not encourage them to pick up the idea and run with it. If they decided to change the way they worked, even in quite small ways, this would affect all their "internal customers". If they then ran a seminar to tell the story, it might give others some ideas.

The Human Resources Department

This has the advantage of being where the people management systems are located – and the reputation for being just as conservative in defence of its own practices as anyone else! People in this function are often knowledgeable about ideas of learning and development, and this can be a great help, especially if they are dedicated to their own learning and development. However, if they are "experts in self-development for others" then paradoxically new initiatives can be blocked.

The change equation

It sometimes takes a shock to shake people or organizations out of the rut in which they are stuck. Suddenly things cannot continue as before. New learning is needed quickly. However, as our colleague John Burgoyne says, change and learning through crisis is painful and wasteful – restructurings, redundancies and so on.

> "Many organizations seem to function rather like a drunk going down a corridor. They set off in a certain direction; after a while they crash into the wall; if they survive they set off in another direction and repeat the process."[3]

It is better to anticipate the need to change, not to wait for the crisis to happen. So companies embark on big change programmes although, as seen in the last chapter, many organization-wide change programmes initiated from the top and cascaded down do not work. Off-the-shelf products are not rooted in real life problems and concerns. Even with well-designed and grounded change programmes there are many things that can go wrong.

The Change Equation sums up what is needed to give any proposed change the chance of working.

$$D + V + M > P$$

Where:

> **D** = the level Dissatisfaction with the current state of affairs
>
> **V** = the desirability of the Vision of the future on offer
>
> **M** = the quality and credibility of the Method or process for getting there.

The sum of these must together be greater than

> **P** = the Pain and cost of change for those concerned.

But waiting for the next crisis to force people to change can be even more painful. The Change Equation does not acknowledge that any change and learning must overcome the P barrier in *everyone* in the company. Everyone's dissatisfaction must be taken into account. Everyone must desire the vision and everyone must think the approach credible – those who are part of the problem must also be part of the solution. For this reason large group events and "whole systems interventions" have become so popular recently.

Taking everyone into account means first valuing each individual, their knowledge, opinions but especially their learning and then developing methods for organizational learning to harness the wisdom of the whole company. Wherever you start, taking a learning approach is inescapably going to change *you*. Change programmes fail because they are designed for *other* people. "Things can't go on like this, they need to change" people say, without any apparent irony. Revans says that successful changes begin with individuals changing and learning about their own practice. His Law of Insufficient Mandate holds that:

> "Those unable to change themselves cannot change
> what goes on around them."[4]

Earlier in this chapter, you checked your organization's readiness to learn. If your organization is ready look at how your organization measures up to the Change Equation. Is there enough dissatisfaction with how things are now? Will this, plus an inspiring vision of the future allied to a workable method for getting there, be enough to overcome the pain or cost of change?

The key to the learning organization lies in the ability and willingness of people to innovate. The speed and effectiveness with which new practice and innovation can spread throughout the organization is also crucial. Ulrich has suggested that the Organizational Learning Capability can be expressed as:

$$OLC = I + G$$

Where

OLC = Organizational Learning Capability

I = ability to Innovate

G = ability to Generalise this learning into good practice throughout the organization.[5]

Being able to innovate obviously depends upon the quality of the people and how good they are at learning and development. Generalising good ideas quickly throughout the organization depends on the effectiveness of communications systems and on the willingness of people to share and exchange ideas. Together these two factors create the Organizational Learning Cycle.

The organizational learning cycle

"Organizational learning occurs when members of the organization act as a learning agents for the organization, responding to changes in the internal and external environments of the organization by detecting and correcting errors in the organizational theory-in-use, and embedding the results of their inquiry in private images and shared maps of the organization."[6]

Nancy Dixon[7] suggests that organizations learn in much the same way as individuals but, because this is a collective process, the learning cycle is more complex. Everyone's active involvement is needed, as is dialogue between all stakeholders, to jointly interpret information about the organization in order to decide on action. This organizational learning cycle is illustrated in Fig. 4 on p.84.

Fig. 4 Organizational Learning Cycle

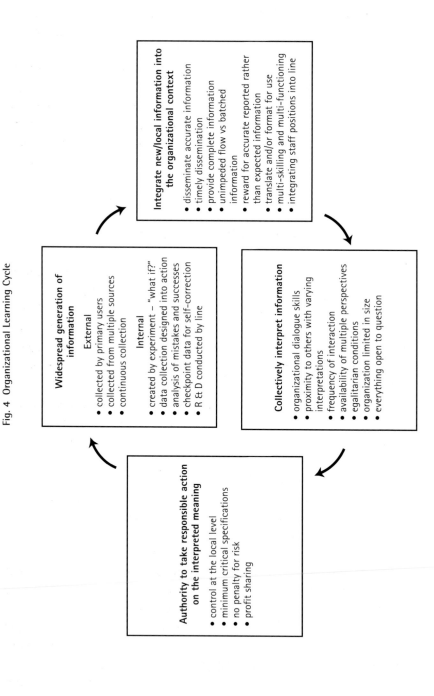

Widespread generation of information

External
- collected by primary users
- collected from multiple sources
- continuous collection

Internal
- created by experiment – "what if?"
- data collection designed into action
- analysis of mistakes and successes
- checkpoint data for self-correction
- R & D conducted by line

Integrate new/local information into the organizational context
- disseminate accurate information
- timely dissemination
- provide complete information
- unimpeded flow vs batched information
- reward for accurate reported rather than expected information
- translate and/or format for use
- multi-skilling and multi-functioning
- integrating staff positions into line

Collectively interpret information
- organizational dialogue skills
- proximity to others with varying interpretations
- frequency of interaction
- availability of multiple perspectives
- egalitarian conditions
- organization limited in size
- everything open to question

Authority to take responsible action on the interpreted meaning
- control at the local level
- minimum critical specifications
- no penalty for risk
- profit sharing

Most of the knowledge about the organization and how to get things done is not available in books or manuals. Rather it is embedded in working contexts – in teams, networks, in the relationships between people – sometimes known as "situated learning" in "communities of practice".[8] Knowledge is socially constructed within work communities and it is only accessible through the process of becoming a member. Individuals learn by taking part, as novices and then co-contributors. These collaborative efforts result in an enhanced general capacity to learn in that particular group.

Learning to learn and learning to change

People's actions depend upon "deeply ingrained assumptions, generalisations, or even pictures or images that influence how we understand the world and how we take action".[9] This notion of mental models or mental maps helps in organizational learning which comes about as people share their individual views, contributing to collective mental pictures of how to get things done here. [10]

Because knowledge is socially constructed and locally situated, what serves well in one organization may not work in another. As a highly-rated executive new to United Distillers (UD) found:

> "He thought that if you pulled a lever at the top, a
> whole machinery would click smoothly into place all
> the way down... in UD, if you pull such a lever it is
> likely to come off in your hand!"[11]

A different mental model would produce a very different action. But the new executive probably did not even know that he held a Lever Model; let alone considered any alternatives. He, as Human Resources Director, wants to build an awareness amongst his colleagues about organizational development in order to help build new companies in emerging markets. They need the skills to enable this process; to influence it but not lead it. His starting questions are:

- How do we make sense of what we do in UD?

- Having made sense of it, how do you influence it?

- How do we understand our own ways of working?

- How can we make more transparent how things get done around here?

- How do we get a good idea to happen?

- How do we improve our effectiveness as a group?

To help with this, he mapped his own mental model about how to get things done at UD, shown in Fig. 5 on p.87.

This mental model starts with an inner idea and spirals out to action. In contrast to the rather mechanical Lever Model, this is more of a Stakeholder Model requiring consultation, dialogue, influence from others at several points. Thinking about the problem from this perspective gives a very different structure of meaning, a very different way to act.

A Community Mental Health Trust in the National Health Service sought to introduce "locality management". Devolving managerial authority to act at local level means integrating the different professional services of health visiting, district nursing and community mental health, which often exist in different compartments with their own rules, cultures and career structures. Here a shared mental model emerged from an organization development project, which responded to the staff's needs and desires to be involved in consultation and dialogue about the change.

Although the cycle illustrated in Fig. 6 (p.88) is also a stakeholder model, it is situated in a particular setting and is very different from the earlier UD example. Nonetheless both show the importance of making organizational processes visible for the purposes of learning. If sharing mental models makes the working and learning processes in the organization transparent then it builds the basis for understanding and improving those processes.

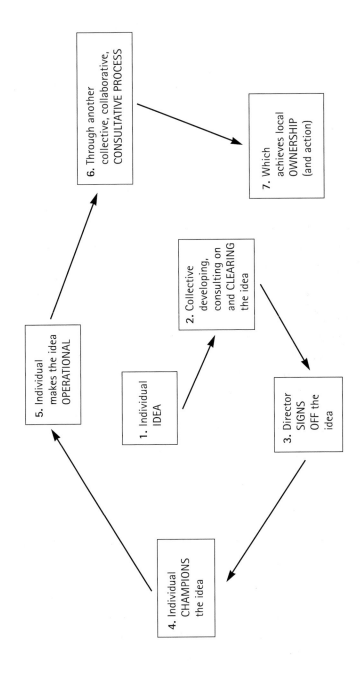

Fig. 5 Stakeholder Model A

1. Individual IDEA

2. Collective developing, consulting on and CLEARING the idea

3. Director SIGNS OFF the idea

4. Individual CHAMPIONS the idea

5. Individual makes the idea OPERATIONAL

6. Through another collective, collaborative, CONSULTATIVE PROCESS

7. Which achieves local OWNERSHIP (and action)

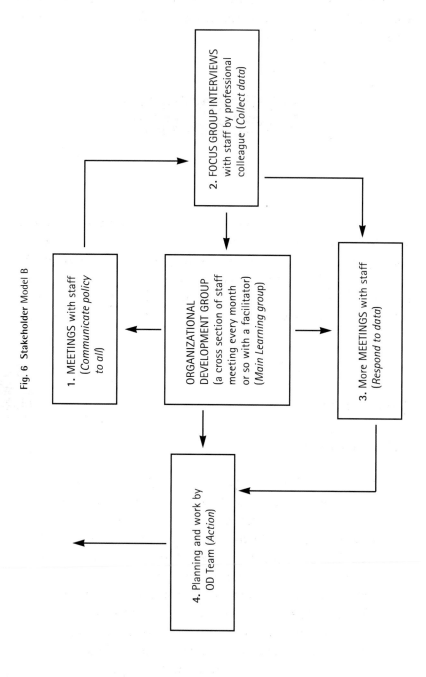

Fig. 6 **Stakeholder** Model B

One way of starting on this is to draw a picture of the way things get done in your organization. Activity 8 will help with this. Turn now to:

ACTIVITY 8 Page 146

It is the learning *process* of becoming a learning organization that is perhaps the most important aspect. As we have said, it is more a journey than a destination – it is how you do it that counts. An organization which demonstrates its ability to "experiment on the side" whilst maintaining a highly controlled mainstream business is the Practice Development Unit at Seacroft Hospital in Leeds:

CASE STUDY

Seacroft Hospital

The Practice Development Unit (PDU) is based in three medical/elderly wards at Seacroft Hospital. It aims to develop multi-disciplinary working amongst the therapists, nurses, doctors, managers and other clinical professionals to promote improved patient care. As part of this the PDU has developed joint projects and practical working partnerships with local academic institutions.

As the result of an earlier merger of St George's, an institution for elderly, long-stay patients, and the Department of Medicine at Seacroft, all PDU staff had to learn to work with more critically ill patients of all ages and in wards with a much more rapid turnover. Some staff found these changes difficult. They felt de-skilled and lost confidence.

The Clinical Director and the Patient Services Manager took action to build skill and confidence in staff through teamwork, de-emphasising professional barriers with a strong, unifying focus on the needs of patients. A flatter structure helped break down the old hierarchical traditions of the NHS, and traditional attitudes such as, "I know my place and it's not for me to suggest ideas but the job of those above me". Staff of all grades and disciplines have been encouraged to take part in decisions and to take a questioning attitude to work.

Risk taking is normally discouraged in hospitals by tight procedures. These also discourage creativity, however, and they have been loosened to promote "well considered risk taking" at all times. The PDU sets out to provide a learning environment in which all staff are encouraged to examine and develop their practice by:

- adopting a supportive management style which facilitates decision making at all levels

- vigorously supporting the personal development of all staff, who have their own learning contracts and who are encouraged to identify and develop areas for research and development for themselves

- learning through shared enquiry, the availability of expertise and constructive criticism which crosses professional boundaries

- providing opportunities for free exchange of ideas both inside the hospital and in the wider world of healthcare.

The changes have given patients more responsibility. They are encouraged to take more decisions about their care; for example, patients take part in identifying problems, agree summaries to be used for care plans and hold all their documentation. Their permission is required for anyone else to read them. Clinical jargon has been reduced making treatments more understandable to patients. A Carers' Group, set up by one of the nurses on her own initiative, shows what can be done in this sort of learning environment. Supported and resourced by management, this group has contributed greatly to carers' quality of life.

Despite the general optimism in the PDU a few staff felt that they lost more than they gained. However, most have welcomed the changes which create "a clinical climate which encourages and empowers nurses and therapists to be knowledgeable, reflective and autonomous practitioners who work in harmony together".[12]

•••

For obvious reasons experiments in hospitals are generally frowned upon, and the Seacroft example is encouraging because it shows how even such necessarily rule-bound organizations like hospitals can experiment and improve for the benefit of clients – in this case the patients and carers.

Conclusion

The readiness to learn is an important pre-condition. The focus and direction of any effort to improve an organization's learning will depend upon many unique characteristics including its vision of the future. Understanding the organizational learning cycles and building them into working practices throughout the enterprise brings about the benefits of the learning organization. Encouraging people to share their mental models of how things happen, building and strengthening the collective maps and understandings of what works well in the organization, and, above all, supporting action by everyone to make things better is a sounder way to promote organizational learning than big and expensive "change programmes".

SOURCES FOR CHAPTER 6

[1] Adapted from Pedler MJ, Burgoyne JG & Boydell TH (1997)
The Learning Company : A Strategy for Sustainable Development
Second Edition McGraw-Hill, Maidenhead, UK pp 66-68

[2] Revans RW (1982) *The Origins and Growth of Action Learning*
Chartwell Bratt, Bromley, UK p284

[3] Burgoyne JG (1992) "Creating the Learning Organization"
RSA Journal Vol CXL (5426) p324

[4] Revans RW (1998) *The ABC of Action Learning* Lemos & Crane, London

[5] Ulrich D (1994) in Stewart TA "Your Company's Most Valuable Asset :
Intellectual Capital" *Fortune* 3 October 1994 p72

[6] Argyris C and Schon DA (1978) *Organizational Learning : A theory of action
perspective* Addison Wesley, Cambridge, Mass. p 29

[7] Dixon N (1994) *The Organizational Learning Cycle* McGraw-Hill,
Maidenhead, UK p 70

[8] Drath WH & Palus CJ (1994) *Making Common Sense: Leadership as
meaning-making in a community of practice* Center for Creative Leadership,
Greensboro, N. Carolina.

[9] Senge P (1990) *The Fifth Discipline : The Art and Practice of the Learning
Organization* Doubleday Currency, New York p8

[10] Argyris & Schon (1978) Ch. 1

[11] Pedler MJ & Aspinwall KA (1996) *"Perfect plc?" : The Purpose and
Practice of Organizational Learning* McGraw-Hill, Maidenhead, UK p 94

[12] Adapted from : Chapter 6 of Pedler MJ & Aspinwall KA (1996)

7. Towards the Good Society

IN THIS CHAPTER: What is all this learning for? Each individual or organization exists in a wider context and needs wider purposes beyond survival and self-interest.

Contents

7 Towards the Good Society

"Whether we do well, whether we like ourselves, whether we lead happy and productive lives, depends to a large extent on the companies we choose. As the Greeks used to say, 'to live the good life one must live in a great city'."[1]

In this chapter we consider the wider contribution of the learning organization: what is it for and who benefits? Always in a process of becoming, moving from here to somewhere better, a learning organization looks restlessly for new purposes and directions. This raises deeper questions:

- What is all this learning for?

- What do we want to be next as an organization?

- If we want to better than we are now, what does "better" mean?

- Who benefits from the learning organization?

Such questions move us up rather than down the How/Why Ladder: shown in Fig. 7 on p.98.

The How/Why ladder

Purpose

↑

WHY?

↑

The Learning Organization?

↓

HOW?

↓

Action

Fig. 7 The How/Why Ladder

Most of this book is concerned with the what and the how; what is a learning organization and how is it brought about? Asking *how* focuses attention on action and down-to-earth implementation. But an exclusive focus on the how results in a blinkered view, where blinded by shining visions, people no longer question the purpose of what they are doing. The "Blind Automaton" unknowingly crushes everything in its path and is ultimately doomed.

Whether an individual or a company needs to learn or not is always connected to purpose. People and organizations learn in order to get on with life the best they can. In learning, as the old is discarded to be replaced by the new, questions of identity and purpose are raised. How does this make sense? Asking why also tends to bring in the wider context: How do we fit in with the whole? What is our part?

Take a moment to think about yourself and how you make sense of the world. Do you naturally tend to focus on yourself, your family and the here and now, or do your thoughts and concerns range more widely to the point of considering global implications of your actions?

Activity 9 (Two Perspectives on Life) demonstrates the difference that this can make. Turn now to:

ACTIVITY 9 Page 150

It is hard to hold more than one perspective in mind at a time, though people might move between them depending upon the issue in question. Day-to-day pressures can push towards immediate, individual needs; for example, customers are urged to ask for what they want and to demand the best. At the same time, there is more to life than this consumerist pre-occupation; we want, and are capable of, so much more.

How about your organization? What perspective does it take? Activity 10 poses some questions about the purpose of your organization. Turn now to:

ACTIVITY 10 Page 152

Beyond survival

For many people, the learning organization is about being flexible, adaptive and being in the right place at the right time to take full advantage of change and the opportunities it brings. This is a powerful image but it is only part of a three stage process of developing consciousness in organizations:[2]

- *Surviving* – here the organization forms habits and processes that enable it to carry out the basic task and to deal with any problems in a fire-fighting way.

- *Adapting* – here the organization continuously adapts its habits and procedures, flexing and changing in response to environment trends and forecasts.

- *Sustaining* – here the organization seeks to contribute as well as to gain advantage from its contexts, aiming for a mutual, sustainable relationship with its environments.

Where does your company stand in relation to these aspirations? Asking the question *Why* and considering personal or organizational purposes, is the arena of ethics and moral behaviour. An apparently straightforward question, "Why is the company doing this?" can elicit the equally simple answer – "In order to stay in business". But whilst this is not an immoral answer – businesses like individuals usually want to survive – it does not relieve anyone from moral responsibility. Would you do absolutely anything to survive? If not, then what is it that you would absolutely never do? What is being done now that would not even have been suggested in easier times? And what might be the unintended consequences of the things being done now?

Asking why is often not easy. It may be difficult to raise the issue of ethical behaviour in organizations because not everyone is convinced that it is useful or even possible to do so. A *Financial Times* reviewer describes Charles Handy's call[3] for a more reflective, spiritual approach to business and a move from survival to contribution as "winsome"; unlikely to impress the hard headed.

Tom Lloyd[4] is distinctly instrumental in his approach to business ethics arguing that companies are a non-human life form at an early evolutionary stage. Although he agrees that it can be advantageous to be co-operative, the fundamental purpose of this behaviour is to ensure that your company wins the "tournament". This is a curious use of the term, quite different from the situation where people work co-operatively for the same ends. The "competitive co-operation" of the market place, lauded by economists as the engine of progress, is seldom founded on equal partnership. Where both sides are working to maximise their own interests, one or another is almost always at a disadvantage and is endeavouring to remedy this imbalance. Solomon reminds us that while competition has its virtues it does not automatically lead to development. There is a distinct downside:

> "Rival companies have often competed each other into oblivion. Rival managers bucking for promotion, executives competing for 'the top spot'… have often dragged a whole company down with them.
> Competition too often leads to teleological blindness and replaces the search for excellence with mere desperation."[5]

Though there may seem to be little room for soft heartedness in competitive times, being hard headed can also lead to disaster. The School for Social Entrepreneurs[6] in London, founded by Michael Young, is "for the hard-headed and high-minded". These two positions may more often be seen to be in opposition. One must be one or the other. Hard-headedness increases the chances of individual survival, whilst high-mindedness helps one to do the "right" things. Each also has its shadow; hard-headedness taken to extremes can lead to mutual destruction or the emergence of a sole survivor, high-mindedness to self-denial and self-sacrifice.

Beyond profit

When making profits becomes a sufficient, rather than a necessary, condition for business, it has become an end in itself. Milton Friedman went so far as to suggest that "the social responsibility of business is to increase its profits" but the effects of the downsizing, restructuring and relocating on community and society, mirrored in the company's damaged and demoralised survivors, make it clear that things are not quite that simple. As (the perhaps aptly named) Solomon asks:

> "What happens to loyalty and integrity when every job seems like a temporary position? What happens to

> merit and quality and progress and innovation? What
> do we have left once a company is "lean and mean" and
> survival is the only value" [7]

Hampden-Turner offers nine cogent reasons why the short term pursuit of the 'unicorn' of profit has long-term damaging consequences.[8] These include the fact that the pursuit of profit leads companies to look backwards rather than forwards. The factors that lead to today's profits may not perform the same function in the future. Global communication, protest and interest groups, health scares, for example, can have a dramatic and sudden effect on what the public will or will not buy.

Most importantly in the context of this book, the desire for profit is too narrow a preoccupation from which to learn. Financial matters have also dominated the public services and the not-for-profit voluntary sector in recent years, but here, though providing value for money is clearly important, the lack of an unequivocal bottom line makes life more complicated. These organizations are usually surrounded by many individuals, groups and other organizations who rightly feel they have a strong stake in the function of their services and who cannot be advised merely to take their custom elsewhere.

> "Schools cannot decide to stop educating five year olds.
> The health service cannot refuse to treat patients in
> Sussex. Yet a private company can easily withdraw from
> markets or reduce its project range."[9]

These differing, even contradictory demands can lead public service workers to retreat behind professional expertise or bureaucratic defences. It is rare to find these differences welcomed as a useful stimulus for the development of co-operative learning relationships within the wider community; yet this is now the key to the survival and further development of these services.

Asking *why* leads to longer-term thinking. "If the company does this where will it lead?" The damage caused by short-term thinking, where people or individual organizations act without awareness of the whole, usually falls on the community. One example is the closure through overfishing of the Georges Bank off the coast of Newfoundland. Here fish stocks had dwindled, and those who had continued to fish because they could not afford to stop, have now lost this source of livelihood altogether.

These "tragedies of the commons" can be seen everywhere. They particularly affect land and natural resources such as water, fresh air, flora and fauna, which are part of the common wealth, and they also include depredations on peace, privacy and silence. The need to safeguard and preserve precious environments is increasingly recognised, but not by all. In business life those who build empires by aggressive takeovers and asset stripping are admired by some and make a few enormously rich but leave little of value behind them.

On trust and love in organizations

Trust is still the basis for many daily business transactions:

> "I took my fee to a local bank for transfer to my bank here. Commonplace sort of transaction, but this was one of those occasions when the commonplace suddenly seemed extraordinary. It hit me that I had handed over my fee to a total stranger in a bank I knew nothing about in a city where I knew almost nobody, and those few unworldly to an extreme, in exchange for a flimsy piece of paper with a scribble in a language I didn't understand. What I had going for me, I reflected unworried as I dashed to catch my train for Zurich was a great web of trust in the honesty of business. It struck me with awe how much that we take for granted in business transactions suspends from that gossamer web."[10]

Without these daily acts of trust banking could not work, but banks have lost a wider sort of trust. A friend went to close her account in order to move it to a bank that took an ethical stance on investment. She explained that she had been meaning to take this step since the bank had employed an influential ex-politician part-time on a huge salary to do business deals with what she held to be dubious foreign governments. The bank employee was shocked, "I didn't know we did that… just think what we could have done here with a fraction of that money." He then said that if it was up to him all banks would put ethical considerations high on their list of priorities, "Banks of all things should be pillars of their communities." "Would it help if I write down my reasons for closing the account on the form?" our friend asked, but the employee shook his head sadly, "No, no one who could do anything about it will ever see this form."

Oscar Wilde's *The Picture of Dorian Gray* provides a powerful image of growing decadence reflected in the portrait locked away on the second floor whilst Gray's physical body and beauty remain untouched. In some organizations today almost the reverse seems to have happened. The preoccupation is with the shadows and individuals feel free only to show their ugly and acquisitive faces, able to talk about sex but not about love. Where are the portraits in your organization which show the kindness, the generosity and the hope?

Like most people, the bank employee wants to be part of a respected and worthwhile organization. The need to give and serve is just as strong as the inclination to hold and take. For example, some three million people work as volunteers in the UK, and the idea of public service retains considerable appeal for many – as two recent instances from the UK National Health Service illustrate:

- A newly appointed non-executive director of a Hospital Trust board was amazed by the levels of commitment she found in the staff in the hospital. "In the private sector we strive for this but I have never met anything like it."

- A Health Authority manager was impressed by many things she saw on her placement with a national retail business but realised that she had underestimated the potential of the health service to attract employees, "because we are doing something useful, of real benefit to society."

Altruism is a fundamental and significant human quality. At a seminar, Roger Harrison spoke of the "mysterious operations of love in organizations", which he sees in such things as dedication to workmanship, excellence of performance, ideals of service and contribution as found in mission statements, relationships between mentors and protegés and the comradeship amongst co-workers.[11] At least one participant was stunned: "If I go back and tell my boss I've spent a day talking about love in organizations, he'll have me locked up".

The high value placed on self and self-contained individualism is a particular feature of western society, which has become accentuated in recent years. There are other ways of organizing society which promote more altruism and co-operation. When the Aitukaki people of the Cook Islands caught more fish than they could eat, they "stored it in their neighbours bellies". They shared the hard task of thatching roofs as the only way to get things fixed quickly. The arrival of refrigeration and corrugated iron made co-operation less necessary – and it became much easier to fall out with one's neighbours.[12]

The good company

To paraphrase the Greeks quoted at the start of this chapter, "To live the good life one must live in a good company". The work organization is an important community for many people that helps define the values within which they live their lives. Yet, in terms of the three level classification of learning organizations introduced earlier, what values does this work community uphold? Perhaps survival is all important, or perhaps you are urged to be adaptive, flexible, open to learning and responsive to change? Or, are you proud to be part of an organization that seeks sustainability and a mutually satisfying relationship with its environment and where you, as an employee, are encouraged to give and to contribute as well as to take and to benefit?

For John Morris[13] a good company seeks "mutual advantage" by balancing the interests of all stakeholders. The expectations of investors, customers, employees, managers, suppliers and the public require different sorts of quality service:

- owners seek quality of business performance and quality of management

- consumers want value for money and quality of service

- employees want quality of working life

- public seek an acceptable quality of social responsibility.

In a healthy society, the good company that looks beyond itself to the wider community, seeking to contribute to the needs of a widening group of stakeholders, is the only organization fit for the employment of good citizens.

Are all learning organizations good companies?

So, is a learning organization automatically a good organization? Almost certainly not. An organization could be well aware of its learning processes and leveraging a good return from them and yet still be pursuing narrow and "selfish" ends. Where would you place your company on the grid[14] shown in Fig. 8 on p.107?

The grid shows that the two dimensions of being ethical and being "learning-full" are not necessarily correlated. We might wish that all learning companies were also "good companies" or that all companies pursuing noble ends were also aware of and fully utilising learning at individual, team and organizational levels to further improve their performance. This is often not the case,

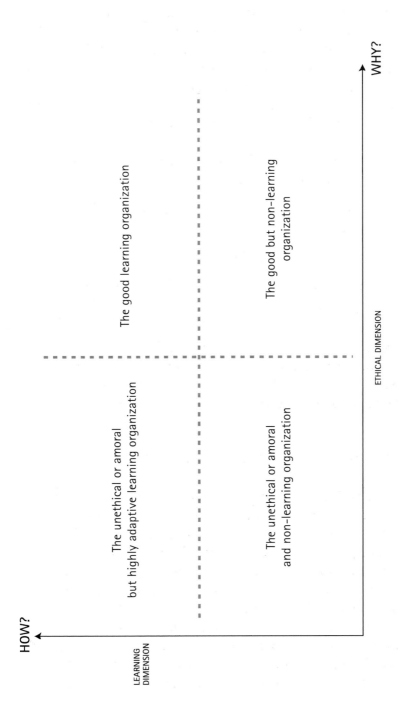

Fig. 8 Learning and Ethics

however; narrowly focussed companies who are capable of acting rapaciously may demonstrate an impressive ability to learn and adapt quickly to new circumstances and opportunities. Equally, organizations set up to pursue the good can rely too much on the unifying and committing effects of such worthy ends and find it almost impossible to change.

Balancing learning with worthwhile purposes is continuously difficult, and is unlikely to remain resolved in any organization for long. However, this is a moral debate, which affects everyone who works in the company or is touched by its activities. Our plea here is for that debate and argument to be given permission and space to take place in the context of the purpose of all organizations seeking to improve their performance and contribution.

CASE STUDY

Traidcraft and social accounting[15]

One organization which tries to live out the ethic of the good learning organization is Traidcraft, which is dedicated to fair trading and to placing the needs of suppliers alongside or even above the needs of customers and shareholders. Ethical businesses such as Traidcraft work on the belief that people want to deal with and buy from them because they share the same concerns and values.

Founded in 1979, Traidcraft works with over 100 overseas suppliers from 26 countries in Asia, Africa and Latin America. It employs some 150 people at its head office and warehouse in Gateshead selling imported handicrafts, clothing, books, cards and paper products, tea and coffee through a network of some 2,000 volunteer representatives and retailers. A distinctive set of values, drawn from its Christian roots, guide day-to-day business activities. Traidcraft's mission – "trading for a fairer world" – aims at "the promotion of greater love and justice in the trading process."

"Traidcraft is not a charity; we're a growing business enterprise. We are not just selling goods; we're challenging the way the rich exploit the poor. We are demonstrating that trade with developing countries can and should be based on justice, concern for people, partnership between rich and poor and care for the environment."

As part of the Fair Trade Foundation with its pioneering "Fair Trade Mark" logo, much of Traidcraft's campaigning and educational purpose is done in collaboration with other organisations. Cafédirect Ltd is one such collaboration with Oxfam and others, which has managed to get fairly traded coffee on the shelves of the big supermarkets and make an impact on the UK's £600 million coffee market.

Traidcraft's annual Social Accounting Report examines the perspectives of all stakeholders, including shareholders, producers, suppliers, staff, voluntary representatives and retailers, the wider public and environmental aspects, on the social, economic, ethical and even spiritual effects of its business activities. The social accounting process ensures that the company does not become complacent by listening to all those in its network of business partners and weighing their views against the quality framework and the foundation principles and values. This social auditing process is also Traidcraft's principal vehicle for learning as a company:

"We've made an investment in time and resources into something which is helping us corporately learn about Traidcraft. Without the Social Accounting Report we'd just read our glossy annual report – read it, love it, get on with the work. What's happening now is that through the year we're quoting the Report to ourselves, talking about what shareholders said about us, what producer partners said. I've only seen a snippet of what's being done this year and already it's bringing out huge questions... not only in tangible things such as developing non-financial performance indicators but also our day-to-day activities, it's coming up all the time and is very closely linked to our corporate learning."

On being hard-headed and high-minded

Traidcraft is a somewhat unusual company – one audit showed that it was overlooking the interests of its shareholders. Just because those who had provided initial capital had foregone the right to financial interest, this did not mean that they were without needs. Indeed it turned out that they felt somewhat neglected and wanted to be kept informed, recognised and appreciated – a social audit finding which was quickly acted on. The shareholders have also criticised the company for maintaining its faith with suppliers and not acting quickly enough to safeguard profit in the face of falling demand for certain goods.

Being too high-minded and insufficiently hard-headed enough for its own long term interests is perhaps an unusual type of error, yet it happens. People and organizations make their own peculiar choices, including those of self-sacrifice, but all share the experience of having to make difficult decisions between self-interest and best ethical practice. Hard-headedness and high-mindedness often appear as opposing positions – to choose one is to incur cost or loss in the other – but they are really the horns of a dilemma. As Charles Hampden-Turner has suggested, the task is to hold them both in mind whilst steering a course that takes account of both high standards and the bottom line, as illustrated on the next page.

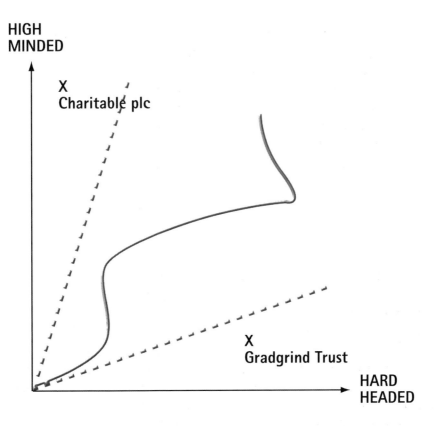

HIGH MINDED

X
Charitable plc

X
Gradgrind Trust

HARD HEADED

Activity 11 invites you to plot the course your organization is taking. Turn now to:

ACTIVITY 11 Page 154

There is evidence that the wider concerns of the "good company" are gaining ground in the mainstream business community. Those who hold that "the business of business is business" and nothing more are under pressure to recognise a wider range of stakeholders including ecological and human rights interests. In pursuit of hard-headedness as well as high-mindedness, the "Balanced Scorecard" notion puts measures of customer satisfaction, internal operations, innovation and organizational learning alongside those of financial performance.[16] Measures such as these are a concrete way of recognising the voice of stakeholders and the bigger and more influential the organization, the more of these it has. The good company is still self-interested of course, but in an enlightened way and increasingly in partnership with all those with an interest in its performance and future.

Company to community: whole systems development

The significance of stakeholder approaches for developing both social responsibility and organizational learning, is reflected in the growing popularity of large group interventions where whole organizations or communities meet to discuss progress and plan the future. Whole systems approaches are based on "search conferencing", which can involve everyone, or at least their representatives, in collective analysis, planning and action. Weisbord describes this as, "getting everybody into improving the whole" and as the culmination of an historical learning curve of social action:

1900	Experts solve problems
1950	Everybody solves problems
1965	Experts improve whole systems
2000	Everybody improves whole systems.[17]

In whole systems development, large numbers of people engage in face-to-face dialogue with each other and with the leaders of the organization or the community. The purpose is to ensure that everybody sees the big picture, has a hand in creating an agreed vision for the future, and starts to align their own actions, along with those of colleagues, to bring this into being. If leaders are prepared to be open and experimental, these events create temporary organizations in which people can experience different relationships with one another.

One account of the whole systems development in action in Walsall in the UK specifies five "keys" to the process:[18]

Getting the whole organization into the room together

Anyone who is part of the problem or will be affected by a change should also be an architect of that change. "Big Events" can involve hundreds of people grouped around tables representing the views of all organization or community members and stakeholders.

Public learning

This approach derives its power from public evidence of learning and commitment from "everyone in the room". People hear colleagues from other departments make action plans to change relationships; everyone sees community leaders or senior managers being questioned on their policies and receiving feedback, which often leads to changed direction. This needs effective preparation by a number of teams including a leadership team to give overall leadership and direction to the change; a design team of representative members to develop the design of the change process and also a consultant's team to guide the change process itself.

Diversity

The full diversity and complexity of the system should be represented and be present in the room together. The full range of grades, departments or professions in a company, of social groups in a community, all differences by status, gender, ethnicity, age and any other relevant voices such as stakeholders and service users are included.

Effective small group working

Participants work in "max-mix" (maximum mix) groups to give the widest opportunities to speak and to listen to the views and ideas of others; and also in action groups to deliver the agreed agenda.

Follow through

These "Big Events" produce great energy, commitment and heady expectations. The importance of Follow Through can scarcely be over-emphasised. The creation of "exit strategies" must precede any Big Event and the resources for continuing support for action and learning must be secured. These will enable the new ways of doing business and delivering services generated by the process to be brought to life.

Developing the good society

What is the point of creating strong and effective learning organizations unless they can share and spread their learning and its benefits to the communities they serve? Already divided on the basis of those who are employed and those who are not, neighbourhoods may become even more polarised if businesses and organizations only focus on survival and adaption to maximise narrow ends. A recent report talks of the "breakdown of civil society" in the UK:

> "In one study conducted for Newcastle City Challenge by Blake Stevenson Ltd, residents described one area as a 'war zone'. Burglaries, car crime, violence, threatening behaviour, all night parties, drunkenness in the street were the norm. Problems were caused by a minority of 29 residents from 13 families who together possessed 395 convictions. Sixty Asian households were the first to leave, but others followed suit. One young family called the police after their fourth burglary. Minutes after the Panda car had left, all the windows in the house were smashed. This family fled the area, for the sake of their mental health, leaving behind a house that was virtually valueless despite it having a £25,000 mortgage."[19]

A lot needs to change in the way we do things. Working in a way that recognises all stakeholders and that seeks to develop the whole system makes great demands upon organizations and their leaders – which many may not be willing or able to meet. Public service organizations have the most obvious cause to seek radical participation and transformation in their role as agencies that seek to improve and develop communities. But public service is not confined to the public services. Ambitious leaders in business and all types of organizations can set good examples of "public learning", without which lasting change and development is unlikely to happen.

Fat chance, you may say. Well, it is asking a lot. But the desire to improve service and quality in the public services must be achieved with finite, often declining resources and in the face of increasing and competing demands from service users. And in the commercial sector, rapid change, inexorable competitive pressures, increasingly demanding customers and infinitely unpredictable futures equally call for drastic measures. In such circumstances, engaging with the conflicting demands of multiple stakeholders, working with anybody with an interest in the company – however negatively this may be expressed initially, offers "breakthrough" possibilities which cannot to be achieved by more incremental means.

The "good" learning organization seeks to develop and transform itself by drawing on the intelligence and variety of all its members, including its diverse stakeholders. Such an organization seeks to develop its members and its learning processes to make collective meaning and take concerted action towards desired ends – which include the type of community and society we would all like to live in.

Who has a stake in, and who benefits from the activities and outputs of your organization? And in what proportion? Turn now to:

ACTIVITY 12 Page 156

SOURCES FOR CHAPTER 7

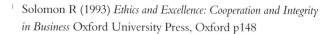

[1] Solomon R (1993) *Ethics and Excellence: Cooperation and Integrity in Business* Oxford University Press, Oxford p148

[2] Pedler MJ, Burgoyne JG & Boydell TH (1997) *The Learning Company : A strategy for sustainable development* Second Edition McGraw-Hill, Maidenhead pp 4-5

[3] Handy C (1996)*The Search for Meaning* Lemos & Crane, London

[4] Lloyd T (1990) *The Nice Company: Why nice companies make good profits* Bloomsbury, London

[5] Solomon R (1993) *Ethics and Excellence: Co-operation and Integrity in Business* Oxford University Press, Oxford p5

[6] School for Social Entrepreneurs 18 Victoria Park Square, London E2 9PF

[7] Solomon R (1993) p5

[8] Hampden-Turner C (1990) *Charting the Corporate Mind* Blackwell, London

[9] Haigh D (1993) "The Business Environment of the Twenty-first Century" quoted in Pedler MJ and Aspinwall KA (1996)

[10] Jacobs J (1992) *Systems of Survival : A dialogue on the moral foundations of commerce and politics* Hodder & Stoughton, London p5

[11] Harrison R (1995) "Leadership and Strategy for a New Age" in *The Collected Papers of Roger Harrison* McGraw-Hill, Maidenhead pp 165-182

[12] In Bottery M (1992) *The Ethics of Educational Management* Cassell, London p 87, quoting Graves and Graves (1983) "The cultural context of prosocial development : an ecological model" in Bridgeman DL (Ed) *The Nature of Prosocial Development* Academic Press, New York

[13] Morris J (1987) "Good Company" *Management Education and Development* 18(2) pp 103-115

[14] From Pedler, Burgoyne & Boydell (1997) p91

[15] Adapted from Pedler MJ & Aspinwall KA (1996) pp161-167

[16] Kaplan RS & Norton DP (1992) "The Balanced Scorecard : Measures that Drive Performance" *Harvard Business Review* 70 (1) Jan/Feb pp71-79 & Kaplan RS & Norton DP (1993) "Putting the Balanced Scorecard to Work" *Harvard Business Review* 71 (5) Sept/Oct pp134-147

[17] Weisbord MR (1992) *Discovering Common Ground* Berrett-Koehler, San Francisco. Also, Weisbord MR & Janoff S (1995) *Future Search : An action guide to finding common ground in organizations and communities* Berrett-Koehler, San Francisco

[18] Wilkinson D & Pedler MJ (1996) "Whole Systems Development in Public Service" *Journal of Management Development* 15 (2) pp 38-53

[19] Knight B & Stokes P (1996) *The Deficit in Civil Society in the United Kingdom* Working Paper No 1, Foundation for Civil Society, Birmingham pp 19-20

8. Activities

The twelve Activities are designed to apply the learning organization ideas in practice.

Activity 1: Ages and Stages[1]

Living organizations have a biography from birth, through various stages of development and finally to death. Organizations are formed by their:

Ideas - the visions and images that founders seek to realise and that are passed on to succeeding generations to re-create

Phase - the life stage of the company, for example, infant, pioneer, rational, overripe bureaucracy, dying

Era - the economic, social, political and cultural context.

Ideas are the major source of an organization's difference and "personality". Even when they are in the same business, organizations are built on different core ideas and purposes. The current era for most organizations is one of competitivenss and unprecedented change. The phase of development of an organization is one source of difference. It is common to describe organizations as if they were people - as being strong or weak, young or old, informal or cold.

Like people, some organizations, vibrant and dynamic in their youth, get stuck and lose their way, whilst others manage to renew their energy and purpose. Looking at the organization as a unique culture or "personality" helps with thinking through what needs to happen next.

From Pedler MJ and Aspinwall KA (1998) *A Concise Guide to the Learning Organization*, Lemos & Crane, London

Ignoring for the moment your organization's actual age, which of the following would you say best characterised its current stage of development:

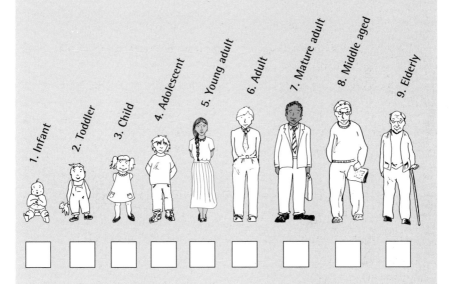

Thinking about the biography of your organization - in what ways has it transformed itself? What evidence is there of "historic organizational learning"? The questions might help you to think about this:

1. Think of the organization as it was five or ten years ago , what stage was it at then?

2. Now, imagine it five or ten years in the future , what will it be then?

3. Is your organization developing or is it just getting older?

From Pedler MJ and Aspinwall KA (1998) *A Concise Guide to the Learning Organization*, Lemos & Crane, London

Activity 2 : Defining Your Learning Organization

This Activity is designed to help identify and create a definition of the learning organization to suit your unique situation.

You can do this alone, but it is probably better in company with a few other people or even with a much bigger group (large numbers of people can be involved through whole systems development events as described in Chapter 7). For the purposes of this activity now, we will assume that you are doing it alone or in a small group.

1. First of all, brainstorm how your organization would be - what it would look like, feel like, and how would it act - if it was a learning organization.

Write your ideas or statements on Post-its and stick them up on a flipchart or wall.

2. Now forget about your ideal picture for the time being and brainstorm your idea of a NON-learning organization.

You can have some fun here by recalling all the situations you have been in where learning was avoided, prevented or crushed, where mistakes were covered up, where people were blamed for speaking the truth, rewarded for resisting innovation and so on. Let yourself go!

As before, write your ideas or statements on Post-its and stick them up on a flipchart or wall.

From Pedler MJ and Aspinwall KA (1998) *A Concise Guide to the Learning Organization,* Lemos & Crane, London

3. Now look at both sets of statements - what must and what must not be there in your ideal learning organization? Sort your Post-its into these three groups:

MUST be there

COULD be there

MUST NOT be there

Sometimes visions are easier to arrive at by deciding what you don't want as much as by what you would like to see there. These are the "noxiants" - poisons which will kill off your vision before it can be realised.

4. Finally tidy up your MUST list (including any COULDs you want) to complete the following sentence in as few words as possible whilst capturing your key ideas or statements:

"In

(Your organization's name)

what we mean by the learning organization is...

From Pedler MJ and Aspinwall KA (1998) *A Concise Guide to the Learning Organization*, Lemos & Crane, London

Activity 3 : How does Your Organization Measure Up?

This Activity enables you to check how your organization measures up to the Eleven Characteristics of the Learning Company.

You can do this alone of course, but it is far better to involve some other people in the exercise, for then you have the opportunity to discuss where you agree and disagree, which is the best way of making the use of this sort of model.

Another way to use this activity is as a survey before holding a discussion on the topic. Distribute the questionnaire to all the people in a team, department or whole organization, collect the anonymous replies, score them and then feed them back as a way of starting the discussion. This might lead to some good ideas for improving the learning in your organization.

The 11 Characteristics of the Learning Company Questionnaire

Give your organization a score out of 5 for each of the statement listed below. Giving 5 points to any question that would mean that your organisation is very much like this; a score of 0 or 1 would suggest that it is not much, or never like this.

1. We regularly examine the social, economic, political and market trends which affect our business. ☐

2. Everyone here plays a part in policy and strategy formation. ☐

From Pedler MJ and Aspinwall KA (1998) *A Concise Guide to the Learning Organization*, Lemos & Crane, London

3. Access to organizational information and data bases is open to all. ☐

4. The financial consequences of actions are fed back to those concerned as soon as they are known. ☐

5. Departments and units understand each other's purposes and values. ☐

6. There are many different ways of rewarding good work, monetary and non-monetary. ☐

7. Structures are very flexible and change frequently to suit different tasks and purposes. ☐

8. People bring in and share information about what's happening out there from our customers, business partners and so on, as a way of life. ☐

9. We engage in joint ventures to develop new services and to learn about new methods and ideas. ☐

10. People are not blamed for raising bad news. ☐

11. Everyone is encouraged to learn new skills and abilities. ☐

From Pedler MJ and Aspinwall KA (1998) *A Concise Guide to the Learning Organization*, Lemos & Crane, London

12. We find new directions by experimenting with practice and by setting up pilot projects. ☐

13. Important policies are widely discussed before they are adopted. ☐

14. Information technology really helps us to do new things together and is not just seen for automating processes. ☐

15. People understand the importance of money and resources and also how such things work in this organization. ☐

16. Different sections and units share information and skills and help each other out as a matter of course. ☐

17. Most people have a say in the nature and shape of reward systems. ☐

18. People are encouraged to come up with different ways of organizing work. ☐

19. There are effective channels of communication for collecting and sharing information from outside the organization. ☐

 From Pedler MJ and Aspinwall KA (1998) *A Concise Guide to the Learning Organization,* Lemos & Crane, London

20. We often meet with other organizations in our business to share ideas and practices. ☐

21. The central focus of our appraisals is the exploration of the person's learning and development needs. ☐

22. There are lots of opportunities, materials and resources available for everyone's learning on an "open access" basis. ☐

Scoring

Now find your scores by adding the responses to two questions for each of the 11 Characteristics of the Learning Company. For example, Characteristic 1 - a learning approach to strategy - is scored by adding together the points for Q.1 + Q.12

TOTALS

1. A learning approach to strategy
   add **Q.1 + Q.12** = ☐

2. Participative policy making
   add **Q.2 + Q.13** = ☐

3. Informating
   add **Q.3 + Q.14** = ☐

From Pedler MJ and Aspinwall KA (1998) *A Concise Guide to the Learning Organization*, Lemos & Crane, London

TOTALS

4. Formative accounting and control
   add Q.4 + Q.15 =

5. Internal exchange
   add Q.5 + Q.16 =

6. Reward flexibility
   add Q.6 + Q.17 =

7. Enabling structures
   add Q.7 + Q.18 =

8. Boundary workers as environmental scanners
   add Q.8 + Q.19 =

9. Inter-company learning
   add Q.9 + Q.20 =

10. A learning climate
    add Q.10 + Q.21 =

11. Self-development opportunities for all
    add Q.11 + Q.22 =

From Pedler MJ and Aspinwall KA (1998) *A Concise Guide to the Learning Organization*, Lemos & Crane, London

Analysis

Looking at the scores, what do you see? Typically there will be a range of scores, with the organization scoring higher on some items than on others. This is where it is useful to have some discussion in order to make sense of what these scores may mean. Do these high and low scores represent your strengths and weaknesses as a learning organization?

Are there weaknesses that you would like to improve on or strengths that you wish to build up further?

From Pedler MJ and Aspinwall KA (1998) *A Concise Guide to the Learning Organization*, Lemos & Crane, London

Activity 4 : Learning at Work

Here is an Activity about your own individual learning at work and how it links to the wider organization. Learning in the organization starts with you.

1. Think of a time at work in the last six months or year when you learnt something about yourself, the work that you do, or your colleagues. This doesn't have to be a major event but it must be something that has created at least a small change in you - in what you know, what you do, how you see things and so on.

When you have thought of such a **learning** event, ask yourself:

• What did I learn?

• How did I learn it?

• Which factors helped me to learn?

• What changed as a result? (How do I know that I have learned?)

From Pedler MJ and Aspinwall KA (1998) *A Concise Guide to the Learning Organization*, Lemos & Crane, London

2. Now think of a time when you **resisted** learning, for example, by ignoring feedback or by not accepting suggestions from a colleague. Perhaps you persisted in doing something your way when others had adopted different methods? Or perhaps it was because learning is not encouraged or rewarded where you work? Or maybe because you don't have the time? When you have thought of a recent **non-learning** event, ask yourself:

• What did I resist?

• Why did I resist?

From Pedler MJ and Aspinwall KA (1998) *A Concise Guide to the Learning Organization,*
Lemos & Crane, London

3. Now, thinking about both your learning and non-learning, what are the factors that helped or hindered your learning? Include those within yourself as well as those outside:

	Helps	Hinders
In Me		
Outside Me		

From Pedler MJ and Aspinwall KA (1998) *A Concise Guide to the Learning Organization*, Lemos & Crane, London

4. Finally, what has happened to your learning in your organization?

• Who else in the organization knows that you have learned this?

• Has the organization learned from your learning?

Yes, a great deal ☐

Yes, a little ☐

No ☐

Don't know ☐

Activity 5 : Analysing the Learning Style of Your Organization

Apply the five organizational styles, shown below, to your organization to find your strengths and weaknesses.

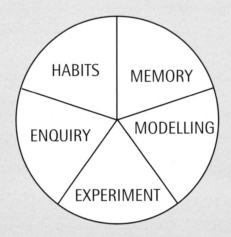

Each of these five organizational learning styles has advantages and disadvantages, which are set out below.

HABITS

Strength = *Good at forming habits and standard operating procedures, which survive the turnover of individuals and are important for long term survival.*

Downside = *The danger of unthinking repetition after the habit has ceased to be functional: the "Blind Automaton" Syndrome.*

MEMORY

Strength = *Good at collecting, storing and disseminating experience, data and knowledge.*

From Pedler MJ and Aspinwall KA (1998) *A Concise Guide to the Learning Organization*, Lemos & Crane, London

Downside = *Can be past-orientated, relying on solutions to yesterday's problems: the "Resistance to Change" Syndrome.*

MODELLING

Strength = *Good at imitating, cherry picking and benchmarking best practice, internally and externally.*

Downside = *A danger of over-valuing external ideas leading to a lack of belief in our ability to innovate internally: the "Others Lead, We Follow" Syndrome.*

EXPERIMENT

Strength = *Strong on innovation, trial and error, and active experimenting with new ways of doing things.*

Downside = *The risk of fixing what "ain't broke", of having too many ideas and a preference for experiment over production: the "Flavour of the Month" Syndrome.*

ENQUIRY

Strength = *Good at reflecting on experience, being open-minded and curious, with a wide awareness of the organization, its context and environment.*

Downside = *Too much enquiry can lead to a loss of focus and lack of attention to detail: the "Ivory Tower" Syndrome.*

Balance is a sign of health in relation to the five organizational learning styles. How does your organization match up?

From Pedler MJ and Aspinwall KA (1998) *A Concise Guide to the Learning Organization*, Lemos & Crane, London

Complete the following sentence for each of the four questions below:

"In terms of the Five Organizational Learning Styles, we are

1. best at: (i)

and next best at   (ii)

2. worst at: (i)

and next worst at   (ii)

From Pedler MJ and Aspinwall KA (1998) *A Concise Guide to the Learning Organization*, Lemos & Crane, London

3. most endangered by the "

Syndrome"

4. most in need of

to improve learning in the organization.

From Pedler MJ and Aspinwall KA (1998) *A Concise Guide to the Learning Organization*,
Lemos & Crane, London

Activity 6 : The Organizational Toxicity Index (OTI) [2]

How toxic is your organization? This Activity measures the health or toxicity of your organization.

For the following ten questions choose one of the responses - (a), (b) or (c) - on the basis of which is most true of your organization, in your experience, for most of the time.

In my organization:

1. Sexist and racist remarks are commonplace and tolerated by management.

    (a) This is not a problem. ☐

    (b) This is something of a problem. ☐

    (c) This is a big problem for me and others. ☐

2. Praise is much rarer than criticism.

    (a) This is not a problem. ☐

    (b) This is something of a problem. ☐

    (c) This is a big problem for me and others. ☐

3. You get little information about your own performance.

    (a) This is not a problem. ☐

From Pedler MJ and Aspinwall KA (1998) *A Concise Guide to the Learning Organization*, Lemos & Crane, London

(b) This is something of a problem. ☐

(c) This is a big problem for me and others. ☐

4. There is competitive pressure from fellow employees to work long hours.

    (a) This is not a problem. ☐

    (b) This is something of a problem. ☐

    (c) This is a big problem for me and others. ☐

5. There is little concern shown for members' health and welfare.

    (a) This is not a problem. ☐

    (b) This is something of a problem. ☐

    (c) This is a big problem for me and others. ☐

6. Making admissions of mistakes or failure is "career limiting".

    (a) This is not a problem. ☐

    (b) This is something of a problem. ☐

    (c) This is a big problem for me and others. ☐

From Pedler MJ and Aspinwall KA (1998) *A Concise Guide to the Learning Organization*, Lemos & Crane, London

7. All management decisions are justified in terms of the "bottom line", that is, solely on financial grounds.

    (a) This is not a problem.

    (b) This is something of a problem.

    (c) This is a big problem for me and others.

8. There are a lot of hierarchical distinctions made in terms of conditions, perks like cars and offices, canteens and so on.

    (a) This is not a problem.

    (b) This is something of a problem.

    (c) This is a big problem for me and others.

9. There is little diversity in management – most are male, white, etc.

    (a) This is not a problem.

    (b) This is something of a problem.

    (c) This is a big problem for me and others.

From Pedler MJ and Aspinwall KA (1998) *A Concise Guide to the Learning Organization*, Lemos & Crane, London

10. **It's very hard to get people to listen to you and
     your ideas.**

    (a) This is not a problem.

    (b) This is something of a problem.

    (c) This is a big problem for me and others.

SCORING

Score 0 for every (a)
    1 for every (b)
    2 for every (c).

The minimum score is 0, the maximum 20.

- If you scored less than 5, then your organization is comparatively
healthy, although there may be some points that need attention.

- If you scored 6 to 12, then your organization is quite toxic - to the
point that many people's performance must be impaired.

- If you scored more than 12, your organization is getting to the
point where it is not fit for human beings to live and work in.
Time to do the decent thing?

From Pedler MJ and Aspinwall KA (1998) *A Concise Guide to the Learning Organization*,
Lemos & Crane, London

Activity 7 : Organizational Readiness to Learn

Like people, organizations vary in their openess or readiness to learn. Some are more closed and wary, others eager to acquire new knowledge and welcome novel perspectives. How open and ready for learning is your organization?

To take a spot check on your organizational readiness to learn circle one of the positions on each of the following five point scales:

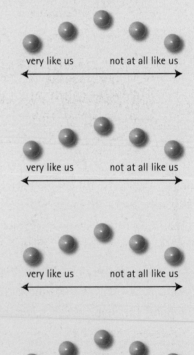

1. We have a strong vision of the future.

   very like us   not at all like us

2. Our vision acknowledges old values and identities as well as new possibilities.

   very like us   not at all like us

3. We involve as many people as possible in the process for arriving at our vision and other key decisions.

   very like us   not at all like us

4. We have a strong interest in the education and self-development of all the people in this organization.

   very like us   not at all like us

 From Pedler MJ and Aspinwall KA (1998) *A Concise Guide to the Learning Organization*, Lemos & Crane, London

5. Learning and contribution rather than position or status are rewarded here.

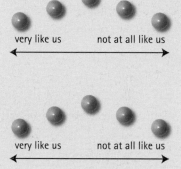

very like us   not at all like us

6. We encourage experiments, pilots, trials as well as being very clear about the need to "stick to the knitting".

very like us   not at all like us

7. We rely a great deal on trusted business partners to deliver our best services and products.

very like us   not at all like us

Scoring

The more ticks towards the left-hand end of the seven scales above, the more likely you are to have the conditions which support further individual and organizational learning. If all your ticks are at the right-hand side, perhaps there is a lot of work to do before you can support the ambition of becoming a learning organization.

However, if all living organizations are learning organizations to some extent, perhaps your right-hand side ticks pinpoint useful areas for action?

From Pedler MJ and Aspinwall KA (1998) *A Concise Guide to the Learning Organization,* Lemos & Crane, London

Activity 8 : Mapping your Organizational Learning Cycle

See if you can draw a picture of how things get done in your organization - not so much how the routine things get done, but how new ideas or practices become accepted. It might help to do this with a colleague.

1. Think of the last time that a significant change of practice or a new idea was established in your organization, or your part of it. Some questions might help to think through the process of how this happened:

- What started the process?
- Who was involved in developing the new idea?
- How were decisions made?
- Who was kept informed?
- Who was involved in implementing the idea?
- What was the sequence of events?

2. Now map or draw the process, using whatever sort of diagram you think fit - algorithm, cycle, fishbone, graph, timeline, zig-zag - whatever best captures the essence of the process.

 From Pedler MJ and Aspinwall KA (1998) *A Concise Guide to the Learning Organization*, Lemos & Crane, London

3. Learning:

(a) How were things different after the new idea compared to before? What was learned?

(b) What sort of "learning process" is apparent here? For example, would you describe it as:

    (i)   Tell and do? ☐

    (ii)   Consult and implement? ☐

    (iii)   Trial and error? ☐

    (iv)   Dialogue and consensus? ☐

(c) What does this tell you about how things are learned around here?

From Pedler MJ and Aspinwall KA (1998) *A Concise Guide to the Learning Organization*, Lemos & Crane, London

Activity 9 : Two Perspectives on Life [3]

Which perspective do you tend to take in decisions that effect you at work or in your life?

The perspective on the left shows a primary focus on the person and the immediate family with the wider world very distant, in small print. The one on the right is a mirror image of this where the primary concern is with the big issues - "What are the consequences, the broader effects, the ultimate outcomes?"

The World/Humanity

The World/Humanity

The Country

The Country

The Local Community

The Local Community

My Organization

My Organization

My Department

My Department

Myself/My family

Myself/My family

From Pedler MJ and Aspinwall KA (1998) *A Concise Guide to the Learning Organization,* Lemos & Crane, London

1. Thinking about these two perspectives, which would you say is most characteristic of you most of the time?

2. So, which one are you most likely to neglect?

3. And, what are the consequences of this for you?

4. What might be the consequences for others?

Activity 10: The Purpose of My Organization

Organizations can have very different purposes: some may exist to make their founders wealthy, some to do good to others, some to make "the best mousetrap in the world". Organizational purposes can also change over time, which is in itself a sign of organizational learning. Those that do not change may need to re-visit their purposes from time to time as part of their vitality and health.

1. When was your organization founded?

2. Why was it founded?

From Pedler MJ and Aspinwall KA (1998) *A Concise Guide to the Learning Organization*, Lemos & Crane, London

3. Is the original purpose still the same today?

4. How is purpose renewed and kept fresh in your company?

5. Who benefits from the outputs of your organization?

From Pedler MJ and Aspinwall KA (1998) *A Concise Guide to the Learning Organization*, Lemos & Crane, London

Activity 11 : Steering a course of high standards and the bottom line

Organizational self-interest and ethical behaviour may at first sight seem incompatible. Is your organization able to steer a course between hard-headedness and high-mindedness?

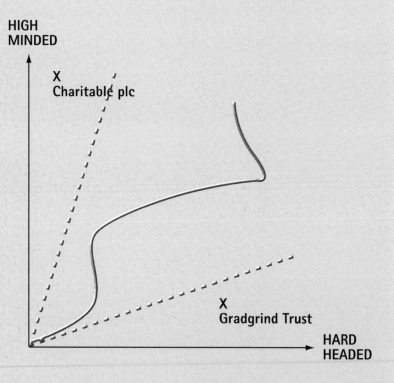

From Pedler MJ and Aspinwall KA (1998) *A Concise Guide to the Learning Organization*, Lemos & Crane, London

On this chart two examples are given of companies consistently choosing one pole or horn of the dilemma over the other.

1. Where would you place your organization in general?

2. Think of a recent choice made in your organization.

Does this represent a "course correction" on the company's part, or is it a "steady as she goes" decision?

Plot this recent choice on the chart. What direction are you headed in? Where should you be heading?

From Pedler MJ and Aspinwall KA (1998) *A Concise Guide to the Learning Organization*, Lemos & Crane, London

Activity 12 : Stakeholder benefits

Consider the following commentary on modern Britain:

> "If the population of Britain were divided according to income, if income were made equivalent to height and if the population then marched past for an hour, it would take a full 37 minutes before the first adult of average height was seen. For the first 15 minutes there would be a parade of dwarves. Stature would increase gradually there after, but 57 minutes would have to pass before we saw people of twice the average height. Giants of 90 feet or more would appear in the last few seconds, with the last one or two literally miles high."[4]

If instead of Britain you were thinking of your company and its stakeholders, how would you arrange them according to relative height?

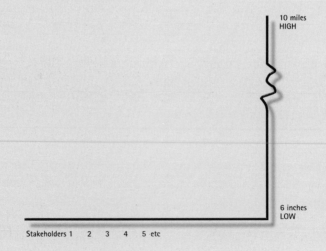

From Pedler MJ and Aspinwall KA (1998) *A Concise Guide to the Learning Organization*, Lemos & Crane, London

What effect do these differences in "height" have upon the way your organization is managed and judged?

What sort of connections and relationships do the various stakeholders to your organization have with each other?

What impact does your organization have on the wider society?

From Pedler MJ and Aspinwall KA (1998) *A Concise Guide to the Learning Organization*, Lemos & Crane, London

SOURCES

[1] Adapted from Pedler MJ & Aspinwall KA (1996) *"Perfect plc?" The purpose and Practice of Organizational Learning* McGraw-Hill, Maidenhead, UK p56

[2] Adapted from Pedler MJ, Burgoyne JG & Boydell TH (1997) *The Learning Company: A Strategy for Sustainable Development* 2nd Edition McGraw-Hill, Maidenhead, UK p153-154

[3] Adapted from Pedler MJ & Aspinwall KA (1996) p202

[4] Hutton W (1995) *The State We're In* Jonathan Cape, London p193

Index

Also published in the Mike Pedler Library

ABC of Action Learning

Professor Reg Revans in this new edition of his classic *ABC of Action Learning* distils the lessons of decades of experience applying the theory he originated - Action Learning - the most important idea to have emerged in management and organizational development since the war. Revans' lifelong mission has been to empower all managers in all organizations to act and to learn from action. The *ABC of Action Learning* sets out practical means of realising his vision. In today's rapidly changing environment where learning is needed to innovate constantly, Revans' ideas are more relevant than ever.

ABC of Action Learning gives you:

- structures to implement action learning programmes based on an understanding of its operational forms

- insights gained from experiences of launching action learning world-wide and responses of top management to efforts to improve their own enterprises

- conditions for bringing about learning in the organization as a whole system.

Professor Reg Revans, creator of action learning, is one of the UK's original business thinkers. A member of the pioneering management team at the National Coal Board after the war, appointed as Britain's first professor of industrial administration in the 1960s, Reg Revans has worked with managers in Britain, Europe, America, Africa and India. He was recently made a Freeman of the City of London.

"interest in Revans' ideas pours in from around the world"
Financial Times

ISBN 1-898001-42-1